ALISTAIR COOKE'S AMERICA

LEVEL II
EDUCATION

ALISTAIR COOKE'S AMERICA

Alfred A. Knopf New York, 1984

Alfred A. Knopf   New York, 1987

This is a Borzoi Book published by Alfred A. Knopf, Inc. Copyright © 1973 by Alistair Cooke.
All rights reserved under International and Pan-American Copyright Conventions. Published
in the United States by Alfred A. Knopf, Inc, New York, and simultaneously in Canada by Random House of Canada Limited, Toronto. Distributed by Random House, Inc., New
York. ISBN: 0-394-73449-1. Library of Congress Catalog Card Number: 73-7268. Manufactured in the United States of America. First hardcover edition published October 22, 1973. First
paperback edition published September 19, 1977. Reprinted Four Times, Sixth Printing,
May 1987.

CONTENTS

For:
Stephen Hearst, who insisted on it
Michael Gill, who saw it through
and
Jane, who suffered it.

Prologue

A PASSAGE TO AMERICA

During the First World War, I was a small boy in Blackpool, a seaside town on the northwest coast of England, which was then the summertime Mecca of the cotton workers of inland Lancashire. It had hundreds of boarding houses and a stretch of sand on which it was possible to drill thousands of soldiers, since it was six miles long and, at the low tide of the Irish Sea, as much as half a mile wide. The town accordingly became a vast cantonment, and pretty soon after the United States declared war in 1917 the "doughboys" arrived. We had seven of them billeted on us. (I learned much later that the men who wrote the American Constitution put in a clause expressly forbidding the billeting of any soldier in a private house. But the Founding Fathers, with their uncanny foresight, saw to it that this prohibition did not apply to England.) I thus had the experience, extraordinary in those days for a provincial middle-class boy, of encountering in the flesh the legendary tribe of "the Yanks," who were known to us only through the silent and often baffling antics of Buster Keaton, Mary Pickford, and William S. Hart at the so-called picturedrome.

The Americans moved in like a football team invading a hospital, for by the autumn of 1917 all the vigorous British conscripts had come and gone from Blackpool, and very many of them were already rotting on the fields of France. They had been succeeded by the last scrapings of the barrel, the old and the chronically frail and sick. All the "C3s," once confidently labeled as unfit for combat and assigned to the auxiliary service of the Royal Army Medical Corps, were now being desperately trained as warriors. To these brave crocks—most of whom would very soon go the way of their comparatively healthy predecessors—were added the "blue-jackets," a legion of the halt and the maimed who would today be categorized by the Pentagon as "impaired combatant personnel" but in those honest days were known as wounded soldiers.

The melding of these convalescents with the bouncing Americans was not easy. Cynical or crippled veterans of Ypres and the battles of the

Somme did not take warmly to eager-eyed youngsters from Iowa and Illinois who announced they had come to win the war so long and inconclusively fought by the British and the French. There was a climactic episode in which a Texan ran into a Lancastrian blue-jacket on Central Pier. They each have their own brand of dead-pan humor unfortunately not recognizable as such to the other. After some dry exchange, the blue-jacket tossed the Texan into the Irish Sea, and for a nervous week or so all the Americans were confined to their quarters. The mordant humor of this situation did not escape a wide-eyed nine-year-old, and so at a tender age I was witness to my first upheaval in Anglo-American relations.

I doubt that I harbored then any preconceptions at all about Americans. Everything about them was peculiar and fascinating. They wore Boy Scouts hats, an oddity that was never explained. All their ranks had identical table manners and, so far as we could tell, identical accents, thereby confronting the British officers with touchy problems in guessing at social station. They treated my mother with a New World courtesy that kept them strangers long after their British counterparts would have been close, if off-hand, friends. But they addressed children as equals, and I was treated as a sort of regimental pet. Since my own father, an artist in metalwork, had been drafted in his fortieth year into an airplane factory in Manchester, from which he came on leave only once a month, I had the luck of having seven extra fathers, and no doubt my inclination to take to Americans was incorrigibly determined then.

They were taller than our soldiers and uniformly paler, almost yellow. I now suppose that they came from the cities of the Eastern seaboard, or perhaps the South, where the burning sun is something you stay away from. At any rate, my father (who had not been to America either) explained to me that their biscuity complexions were due to the famous skyscrapers, which kept the sun off their faces the year round. Later on, after I had been subjected to the only American texts then compulsory in an English elementary school (*The Deerslayer, Hiawatha, The Legend of Sleepy Hollow,* and the totally incomprehensible *Tom Sawyer),* my mental picture of the United States, and of such scattered human life as it supported, became sharper but not, I regret to say, more accurate. First, there was New York, with skyscrapers and yellow men, and red men lurking in the suburbs. Then a long stretch of something called the prairie or pampas (we were never told exactly which) and through the middle of this uninhabited wilderness there flowed a wide river—"the wide Missouri," probably, since that was the subtitle of the only American song we were required to sing in unison. Later still, the musical *Show Boat* came to England and we knew then that the big river was the Mississippi, thrashing with steamboats and gamblers, who were nudged aside from time to time by a man in a white suit and a bushy white mustache who kept rushing to the stern and dropping a plumbline and shouting, "Mark Twain!" Beyond the Mississippi, it was said, there was another yawning prairie rising eventually to the only range of mountains in America, the Rockies; and at last you came on the Pacific Ocean and the only other American city, San Francisco, which we were told had been founded exclusively by Australian convicts.

There was very little in my excellent grammar school education to rip apart this tough patchwork of preconceptions, for in British schools in those days American history stopped abruptly with the outbreak of the Revolutionary War, on the principle that if they didn't need us, we didn't need them. But after the First World War, both the national prejudices I had imbibed and the personal memories of "the Yanks" that tended to contradict them began to blur together and fade as the inevitable reaction against Our Gallant Allies set in. Throughout the 1920s, America became known to us as a lurid society of licentious movie stars, ruthless gangsters, a boastful citizenry, and a grasping government called "Uncle Shylock," who was out to bleed old Europe white with demands for war reparations. Like most healthy schoolboys, I had no more social conscience than a puppy; so that while it was proper to defer to one's parents when they bemoaned the money-mad Republic across the seas and contemplated every American import, from canned beef to shirts with collars attached, as typical bits of "shoddy," these horrors paled for me and my friends before the heroics of Lindbergh, Douglas Fairbanks, and Bobby Jones; the country's reputation for beautiful and pliant females; the arrival of Fred and Adele Astaire; and the joys of American jazz.

This may seem like a very simple load of mental baggage with which a Cambridge graduate was to set sail for the United States in September 1932 after he had been awarded a fellowship for graduate study at Yale. But I believe that the preconceptions about another country that we hold on to most tenaciously are those we take in, so to speak, with our mother's milk; and after the showing of the *America* television series in Britain, it was made plain to me in many penitent letters, some of them from eminent persons, that the infection of these old prejudices is still widespread.

This is not the place to go into all the stages of my subsequent enlightenment, except as they seeded the long, unconscious gestation of this book. My fellowship was intended to train me in the expertise of American theater direction, so as to return and revolutionize the English drama. But one of the "obligations" of my tenure was to be given a car and tour, in the summer vacation, as many of the States of the Union as possible. It was more of an outrageous luxury than an obligation, at a time when bankrupt stockbrokers were pulling their sons out of Yale,

Photographs by Alistair Cooke. New York City, 1942, and New England.

Utah and Kentucky.

and this first safari through America, in the midst of Roosevelt's Hundred Days, shook me out of my deep ignorance of politics. (In those days, a Senator was to me some sort of American with a toga, and for several years such vital mysteries as "judicial review" and "executive usurpation" were meaningless bits of jargon that the newspapers went on about.) But the upshot of this tour was to make the landscape and the people of America far more dramatic than Broadway; and when I returned to England, I weaned myself away from the theater during a tapering-off period as the BBC's film critic and then gave myself over to writing and directing programs about American life and history for a country that was then inadequately informed by a mere handful of correspondents in America, half of them in Hollywood. It was only a matter of time before I returned, on an immigrant visa, and found myself—to my astonishment—launched as a second-string foreign correspondent for the London *Times* and the BBC, required to write and broadcast knowing pieces on the criminal trial of a Tammany leader, the fate of a farm bill, and the indecisive thirteen-hour ordeal of a man waiting to jump from a hotel balcony. During thirty-five years as a foreign correspondent, I must have covered just about everything, from the public life of six Presidents to the private life of a burlesque stripper; from the black market in beef to the Black Panthers; from Estes Kefauver amid the snows of New Hampshire to Jack Nicklaus amid the azaleas of Augusta, Georgia; from Henry Kaiser's Liberty ships to Francis Chichester's *Gypsy Moth* sailing into Staten Island at one in the morning; from the Marshall Plan to Planned Parenthood; from Senator Joseph McCarthy's last stand to the massacre of Muhammad Ali by Joe Frazier.

I list this bewildering variety of assignments without foolish boast, because it is the stimulating duty of a foreign correspondent to cover everything. Whereas a domestic reporter, even at his best, graduates from general reporting and hops up the ladder to success towards a single specialty (sports, organized labor, the stock exchange, or the State Department), a foreign correspondent is required to act on the preposterous but exhilarating assumption that he takes all knowledge for his province and is equally at home in a textile mill, a political convention, a showing of abstract art, a proxy fight, or a launch pad at Cape Canaveral.

In all, I made about a dozen automobile tours of the country, as well as innumerable regional jaunts, and in one long and lonely drive through the late winter, spring, and summer of 1942, as an accredited "war" correspondent reporting from the American grandstand to an audience of embattled Britons, I found myself rediscovering—on re-tread tires at the compulsory thirty-five miles an hour—the whole American landscape, region by region, county by county. The theoretical purpose of this trip was to see and say what the war was doing to such wildly different specialties as steel production, long-staple cotton, the tattooing of sailors' forearms, and the manufacture of heels for ladies' shoes. But what I learned from this memorable experience was that in a continent of (then) forty-eight governments, a half-dozen radically different climates, a score of separate economies, and a goulash of ethnic ingredients, nothing that you say about the whole country is going to be true; and secondly, that the exciting way to learn about the history of this country, and the experience of settling it, is to dig it out of the landscape. It was more fun to come on sheepherders in Idaho talking a peculiar half-Irish, half-Basque lingo than to stay home and read a Congressional report on immigration. A fictional series on, say, "The Forty-Niners" cannot begin to convey the feel of their ordeal as much as a stroll through the graveyards in the foothills of the Sierras.

On all my trips, from the late 1930s on, I packed in an orange crate in the trunk of my car the federal guides to all the states I was likely to drive through. These had been written by penurious writers and local historians enlisted under the Writers Program of the government's Works Projects Administration during the Depression. America, which had had no guidebooks worth the name, suddenly had a library of the best; and it was these unsung historians who put me on to hundreds of places along the road that few tourists had ever heard about. So when the British Broadcasting Corporation first proposed to me the alarming project of recounting the history of the United States on television, I was given the courage, or gall, to attempt it because of two passing thoughts: one was that as a correspondent writing for an innocent audience of foreigners, I usually had to trace the most topical news story back to its historical beginning (you cannot assume, as *The New York Times* must, that its readers can instantly place the history of "interstate commerce" into the context of a sudden violation of it); and through my travels I had acquired something of what Theodore Roosevelt said every President should have, namely, "a sense of the continent." I might not, as many more learned men could, recall at once a well-articulated skeleton of the outline of American history. I had, of course, read a good deal of American history down the years, but when I think of some historic person or episode, I tend to think first of a place, some corner of that continental field that is forever American, because something charming or hideous or otherwise memorable had happened there. So I jotted down a long list of such places, most of them, I should guess, not much known to tourists or even to the standard history books: Catherine, Kansas (the first planting of Turkey Red wheat); Big Bone Lick, Kentucky (the dinosaurs' contribution to "the dark and bloody ground"); New Harmony, Indiana (the most touted of the "communes"); Pittsburg

Landing, Tennessee (the menace of the Union Army's plentiful reserves); The Humboldt Sink, Nevada (the cruelest ordeal of the Gold Rush); Newfane, Vermont (the epitome of native New England architecture); Livingston, Montana (the literal bottleneck in the continental wartime supply route to the Pacific); and so on and on. To arrange these memories of a nation's history from the landscape and not the books seemed the best I had to offer. There are rafts of formidable and brilliant historians. The papers and magazines are groaning with Cassandras. So without any preconceptions about how it would come out (I am not sure whether the United States is going to come out intact or not), I arranged the episodes in chronological order. Whether it was to succeed or fail, it seemed to me a good, though tortuous, thing to attempt: to try and say what is moving about the American experience over four hundred years at a time when that experience is either forgotten, badly taught, or shamelessly sentimentalized; and to recall what is tough and good about the American system of government at a time when that system is poorly understood and, in some high and low places, perilously close to corruption or betrayal.

The nucleus of this book is, of course, the scripts I wrote for the television film. But film has to be direct and immediate, at the expense of reservations and intellectual subtlety. Film as history is therefore inevitably oversimple (still, it is better to be oversimple than overwrought). Complicated issues, such as the scores involved in the making of the Constitution, have to be reduced to dramatic opposites—so that in the fourth episode, for example, the sort of Constitution that was to emerge turned into a clash between George Mason and Alexander Hamilton, with James Madison as the referee and eventual winner. The fourth chapter is considerably longer than the original script and, I hope, truer to the complexities of the seventeen-week debate. Similarly, the Spanish and French contributions, which had to be mercilessly condensed into a single episode, are here given their proper due. In all, this book is about four times the length of the spoken television scripts.

The first thing a foreigner has to try to take in about America—and it is not something automatically grasped even by all the natives—is the simple size of the place and the often warring variety of life that goes on inside it. In a motion picture of the 1930s, the hero was a young American from the prairie arriving in England to take up a Rhodes Scholarship. He settled for his first trip to Oxford into the snugness of an English "railway carriage" and found himself sitting opposite an English parson buried in his newspaper. As the gaping boy looked out over the small-scale landscape with its velvety pasture, the trim spinneys, and the checkerboard hedgerows, he could not restrain himself. "You know, sir," he said, "I guess the whole of England could be fitted into one corner of Nebraska." The parson looked up from his paper and crisply replied, "But to what *end*, young man?"

It is the classic English riposte to the classic American response on first seeing England. From Dickens on, the English have always remarked, with due condescension, on the American preoccupation with size, and the Americans have rarely let them down. And for good reason. If there was one conception more than another that white men had to forget when they came to America, it was of a guaranteed livelihood in a friendly landscape. They had to get used to the idea of a vast and dangerous country whose size alone guaranteed the possibility of success in one part of it after failure in another. The size of the country was the image of their salvation, just as brute size guaranteed sanctuary to the Indians—for a couple of hundred years.

What is consoling about the American concern with size is that once the insular Briton makes the crossing and is exposed to it he tends to share it with a gurgling childlike wonder. In Sussex, he might have been in the habit of driving twenty miles to dinner. But if, like me, he should acquire a friend in some such place as Alpine, Texas, and another in El Paso, he will brag till his dying day that he once drove 360 miles round trip just for a meal. Most people, I believe, when they first come to America, whether as travelers or settlers, become aware of a new and agreeable feeling: that the whole country is their oyster. They may, in fact, settle down in one place and stay there. But America can still fire dull imaginations with the prospect of a continent to explore. In my experience, the only people immune to this vision are those urban types to whom—as the late Fred Allen used to say—"everywhere outside New York City is Bridgeport, Connecticut." This parochialism is common in all the big cities of the East, but in New York City it amounts to a kind of insensate village pride.

There are, in fact, large regions of the United States that will challenge the hardihood of the most carefree wanderer. As I write this, a forgotten skyjacker is either living off roots and mountain-lion meat or, more probably, is frozen stiff on the slopes of the Cascade Mountains. The airplane passenger, on his first flight west, is invariably astonished to look down for hours on a landscape as seemingly hostile as the barren interior of Australia or the craters of the moon. But practically all of it may be driven across comfortably on cement highways and six-lane freeways. The determined adventurer has to make a special effort, if he wishes to imitate the pioneer, and penetrate the Great Basin in Nevada or the fastnesses of the Bitterroot Mountains or the High Sierras.

A famous American historian announced positively in 1893 that the frontier had disappeared three years earlier. But more free land was

Photographs by Alistair Cooke. Kansas wheatfield and Bryce Canyon, Utah.

New Mexico and California.

homesteaded after 1900 than before, and so late as 1927 there were quantities of free government lands available. Undoubtedly, all the land mass of the United States has been mapped, and the prospects for a livelihood in any part of it are known. This is what we really mean by the end of the frontier, the word being taken to bear its original American meaning not of a state or national border but of the unknown land that lay to the west of a fringe of human settlements.

Before we begin to follow the history of the land and its people, it might be well to have in our mind's eye a picture of North America at once sharp and memorable. For a long time, Europeans and Americans alike were stuck with the picture of a giant ray with a shrunken tail curling into the Equator. The projection of Gerhardus Mercator, a Flemish mapmaker, did not allow the lines of longitude to converge at the poles, so the areas near the pole appear wider than they really are, and North America broadens out to the north like an open fan. This causes little confusion to most of us until we hear that the air route from London to San Francisco is shorter over the pole than it is via the Atlantic, New York, and Chicago. For our purpose, what we want is a picture of the terrain as the explorers saw it, then the people who settled it and walked across it, and then went by train, and only in our own time learned less and less of its sweep and character by flying over it.

Fortunately, the broad design was drawn for us, nearly a century and a half ago, by a Frenchman who saw only a little of it from the ground, but he has painted an incomparable big picture of this continent as it may be seen from the godlike height of a space ship. At the very opening of the first chapter of his monumental *Democracy in America*, Alexis de Tocqueville remarks that:

A sort of methodical order seems to have regulated the separation of land and water, mountains and valleys. A simple but grand arrangement is discoverable amidst the confusion of objects and the prodigious variety of scenes.

The continent is divided, almost equally, into two vast regions, one of which is bounded on the north by the Arctic Pole, and by the two great oceans on the east and west. It stretches towards the south, forming a triangle, whose irregular sides meet at length below the great lakes of Canada.

The second region begins where the other terminates, and includes all the rest of the continent. The one slopes gently towards the Pole, the other towards the Equator.

Happily for us all, the United States is a stranger to that "first region" in the North, where there are neither "high mountains nor deep valley," where "great rivers mix their currents, separate and meet again, disperse and form vast marshes . . . and thus, at length, after innumerable windings, fall into the Polar seas."

The second region embraces what is now the United States. It is, Tocqueville succinctly observes, "more varied on its surface and better suited for the habitation of man." So, indeed, it is. Which is why the almost four million square miles of Canada house only twenty-one million people, and the three million square miles of the continuous land area of the United States (excluding the outposts of Alaska and Hawaii) support a population of over two hundred million.

When Tocqueville goes on to describe the land mass of what is now the United States, he sees it very much as an astronaut does:

Two long chains of mountains divide it from one extreme to the other: the Allegheny Ridge takes the form of the shores of the Atlantic Ocean; the other is parallel with the Pacific . . . the vast territory in between forms a single valley, one side of which descends gradually from the rounded summits of the Alleghenies, while the other rises in an uninterrupted course towards the tops of the Rocky Mountains. At the bottom of the valley flows an immense river, into which the various streams issuing from the mountains fall from all parts . . . the Indians, in their pompous language, have named it the Father of Waters, or the Mississippi.

This "grand arrangement" does not take in the Great Basin beyond the Rockies, or the higher range of the Sierras, but it does describe the three commanding features of the whole: the main mountain range of the East, the Appalachians (in his time called "the Alleghenies," because the northern ridge of the chain was most familiar); the largest mountain chain of the West, the Rockies; and in between a huge valley down which "fifty-seven large navigable rivers contribute to swell the waters of the Mississippi" along the twenty-five hundred miles of its course.

These features become very clear on a relief map and compose the big picture: a great quadrilateral, three thousand miles at its widest reach between the oceans, and about twelve hundred miles from the Great Lakes to the Gulf of Mexico. The prime asset of the United States is that it lies between the parallels of 26 and 55 N. Above these limits are bleak and unproductive lands, and below them are tropical forests and deserts and humid climates that debilitate the white man when its diseases do not enfeeble him. On the contrary, the United States spans the limits of the climates that white men can live and work in. The "prodigious variety of scenes" encompasses a widening littoral on the East Coast that goes from skiing country through temperate farmland to semitropical swamps and warm winter resorts; westward, over the Appalachians and across the broadest stretch of land, a huge and fertile prairie rising to the Great Plains; and on the West Coast, from north to south, virgin forest falling away to the green, damp England of Oregon, and down through all the various landscapes of California—Switzerland and Burgundy and Yorkshire and Scotland and Spain—to the desert and the balmy seashore of Lower California.

Although a third of the United States is too cold to maintain dependable agriculture, and a quarter of it is desert-dry, across the rest of the continent the North European was able to grow, and in undreamed-of abundance, every crop he had planted at home and many he hadn't, including maize, cotton, rice, and tobacco. And he was to find here half the world's coal, and more forest and mineral wealth than on any other continent.

The enviable richness of America's natural resources is a theme that Europeans like to dwell on whenever they are feeling peevish about some new American achievement like a moon shot or the fact that more than half the families in the United States have an annual income of $15,000. While the Europeans attribute America's bounty to the luck of her resources, Americans on the other hand like to ascribe it to nothing but character. It usually required a combination of both. As the dramatic history of this country, including the actual invention of a nation, will show.

1
THE NEW-FOUND LAND

Just when America was discovered by the human race is a large puzzle, and a matter of much jealous scholarship. The disputes flare up anew with every unearthing of a skull, a primitive burial ground, a charcoal pit, or a flint knife, and with every fresh scrutiny of an Indian artifact that suggests the symbols or graffiti inscribed in Egyptian tombs or Coptic churches. There are scholars who insist that we cannot know who first began to populate America until we have decided where the human being first appeared on the earth! As late as 1959, it was generally thought that the place was Asia.

In the summer of that year, Dr. Louis Leakey and his wife found two skulls, forty teeth, and a collarbone buried in a ravine on the Serengeti Plain, and thereby not only transferred the origins of man to Africa but set back the date of his appearance by over a million years. It is little wonder, then, that the question of when human beings first embarked for America, or strayed into it, is an open one.

There are eminent scholars who are convinced that America was first seen by Egyptians. There are others who assert the more or less plausible claims of the Greeks, the Etruscans, the Chinese Buddhists, the Hindus, the Japanese, even the Basques—and, of course, the Irish. There are prehistoric mounds in Indiana built, according to the Welsh, by the Welsh. There were early Mormons committed to the belief that the people we call Indians (after Columbus's error in thinking he had come on "the Indies") were descended from the Ten Lost Tribes of Israel.

But since this book is to be about the history of that part of North America that became the United States of America, we must leave these hassles to the archeologists and anthropologists and turn in relief to the present consensus that the first people who saw what we call America were following ice-age mammals who had stumbled east from Siberia into Alaska in search of more food in greener pastures. It was a trek supposed to lead them in time down to the grasslands of the American interior, on east to the Atlantic shores of Canada, south across the

A warrior of the Great Plains: Heap Wolves, a Comanche chief killed by the Osage in 1872, not long after W. S. Soule took this picture of him.

deserts, through semitropical America, and at last to the tip of Chile. Yet fifty-six miles of water separates the Chukchi Peninsula of Siberia from the Seward Peninsula of Alaska. It took sixteen years, two expeditions, and the life of Vitus Bering, a Danish navigator hired by Peter the Great in the early eighteenth century, to conclude that between the two jutting peninsulas, from which today the Soviet Union and the United States of America glare at each other most closely, there was no bridge of land. But there had been, so the accepted theory goes, in the prehistoric time when glacial ice sheets locked up much of our planet's water supply and lowered the level of the sea. Not until about ten thousand years ago, when one of these ice sheets started to melt, were Siberia and Alaska parted once for all by the waters. We can no more than guess how long Alaska entertained the human race, but the appearance of humans south of Alaska is unanimously fixed at a time not later than fifteen thousand years ago.

Unfortunately, American and Russian scientists have lately been pursuing a line of research that may well wreck the "consensus" that the first Americans came from Siberia. While I was at work on this book, I was introduced by Dr. Leon J. Salter to the findings of the American serologist Dr. William Boyd and the Russian anthropologist M. G. Levin, who declare that, while the predominant Asian blood type is B, American Indians run exclusively to A and O. (Other researchers dispute this. Dr. Jack Rogers took blood samples from 87 Aleut Indians and found that though O was indeed most common, two families had types A and B. Rogers's wife, a full-blooded Cherokee from Georgia, has AB.)

We had better simply say that long after man had settled in the land masses of Europe, Asia, and Africa, America was unknown to any human being, but that at some point—we now suppose about fifteen thousand years ago—humans began to range the length and breadth of the Americas. It is the popular belief, handed down to generations of schoolchildren, that Indians were of two main sorts: farmers living in villages or *pueblos*, and hunters—except, of course, in Mexico, where Cortés came on cities of high culture with complicated systems of government not unlike those known in Europe.

In the past forty years, however, anthropologists have done some very thorough digging into the life of the North American Indians and have discovered a bewildering variety of cultures and societies beyond anything the schoolbooks have taught. There were Indian societies that dwelt in permanent settlements, and others that wandered; some were wholly democratic, others had very rigid class systems based on property. Some were ruled by gods carried around on litters, some had judicial systems, to some the only known punishment was torture. Some lived in caves, others in tepees of bison skins, others in cabins. There were tribes ruled by warriors or by women, by sacred elders or by councils, or by fraternities whose rituals and membership were as unknown to the rest of the tribe as those of any college secret society. There were tribes who worshiped the bison or a matriarch or the maize they lived by. There were tribes that had never heard of war, and there were tribes debauched by centuries of fighting. In short, there was a great diversity of Indian nations, speaking over five hundred languages.

For at least a hundred and fifty centuries before "Yankee Doodle," the Indians' way of life composed "the American way of life." It is to most of us a long, dark chapter in American history. And though barrels of lost Egyptian and Asian manuscripts might testify to our ignorant chauvinism, it is the European discovery of America—and the experience of the whites who conquered the continent and settled it—that excites most of us.

So we begin with the simple, colossal question: Who was the first white man to discover America? (It was, incidentally, named after a Florentine businessman and promoter, Amerigo Vespucci, who promoted himself so well that he got his name attached first to South America, and then to the whole continent, though he took no part in the early voyages.) But the first? We simply do not know. The most plausible speculations involve Indian artifacts whose resemblance to the symbols of the ancient civilizations of the Mediterranean Basin can do no more than suggest expeditions of which there is left no trace. But it is certain that the Norsemen, Swedes, and Danes who swarmed over Europe in the tenth century colonized Iceland and Greenland and from there, in the first seven years of the eleventh century, journeyed to the southwest and came on some region of the east coast of North America. Finding "self-sown wheatfields and wild grapes, out of which a very good wine can be made," they called the place Vinland. Throughout the nineteenth century Icelandic scholars debated whether this attractive region lay on the coast of Rhode Island, Massachusetts, Labrador, Newfoundland, or Nova Scotia. The last seems the most likely, though if so its wine industry must have gone into a swift decline.

Lately there has been some powerful propaganda on behalf of the Phoenicians and the Jews, but the records of their voyages are, to say the least, well hidden in the womb of time. It seems sensible to bypass these scholastic brawls and fall back instead on the end of the fifteenth century and Christopher Columbus, and say at once that his first voyage is a decisive event in world history: it brought to the whole of Europe, in the following century, the first shock of recognition that the American continent existed; and it started the adventure that has never stopped since—the exploration, conquest, and settlement of this new-found land.

In 1453, there was a decisive turn in the centuries of warfare between the Christians of Europe and the Moslems of Asia. Their common market, bridge, and gateway was Constantinople, our Istanbul. In 1453, the Turks conquered it, and in so doing shut off the commerce between East and West, the exchange of the cloth, leather, wines, and sword blades of Europe for the silks, jewels, chessmen, and spices of Asia. All things considered, the stoppage was much harder on the court treasuries of Europe than those of Asia and, in one vital item, harder on all Europeans. That item was spices.

Some of the big jolts of history have been caused by the denial of a simple human need. A shortage of water. Lack of bearable living space for a large population cramped in a small country. A total absence of timber, which has plagued the Egyptians since the time of Solomon. But spices? Today only fastidious housewives and food critics for fashion magazines regard spices as fundamental to human survival. The vast majority of ordinary European householders look on nutmeg, cinnamon, cloves, paprika, basil, and the like as gilt on the gingerbread. And many of us, including the Latin nations and the inhabitants of most hot countries, have an incurable hankering after pepper. But in the fifteenth century these—and pepper more than anything—were what made food edible. Salt was available—and the only known preservative—but it didn't do much for food cooked in smoky, open fireplaces. Even in rich houses, the meals came putrid to the table. (Dysentery, by the way, seems to have been considered through most of the last five centuries a hazard as normal as wind and rain.) The spices deceived the palate, if not the digestion, as they sometimes still do.

Spices came from the Spice Islands, which lie east of Borneo and south of the Philippines. We know these islands as the Moluccas, and it is odd that this name should not be as famous in our history as London or Boston. Modern history, you could say, began with the problem of how to bypass Turkey and still get to the Spice Islands of Indonesia—or, more simply still, how to get pepper by sea.

There was a man who believed it could be done and that he had been providentially chosen to do it, although it should be said that his ambitions were a good deal more grandiose than merely the procurement of a cargo of pepper. To appreciate the visionary audacity of this man, to say nothing of his physical courage, we need to examine the only map of the world available to him. It conceived of our planet as a single continuous land mass in the shape—depending on the cartographer—of a pancake surrounded by an unknown ocean, or a giant prawn—a Florida jumbo shrimp—with its two ends enclosing a stretch of that ocean. Flat, in any case. The general belief that the earth was indeed as flat as a pancake implied that beyond the known lands, probably not far out into the ocean, there was nothing but the void of oblivion. Sail to the edge and

This may be a good likeness of Christopher Columbus, but there is no way to be certain. It was painted a few years after his death by the Italian Sebastiano del Piombo.

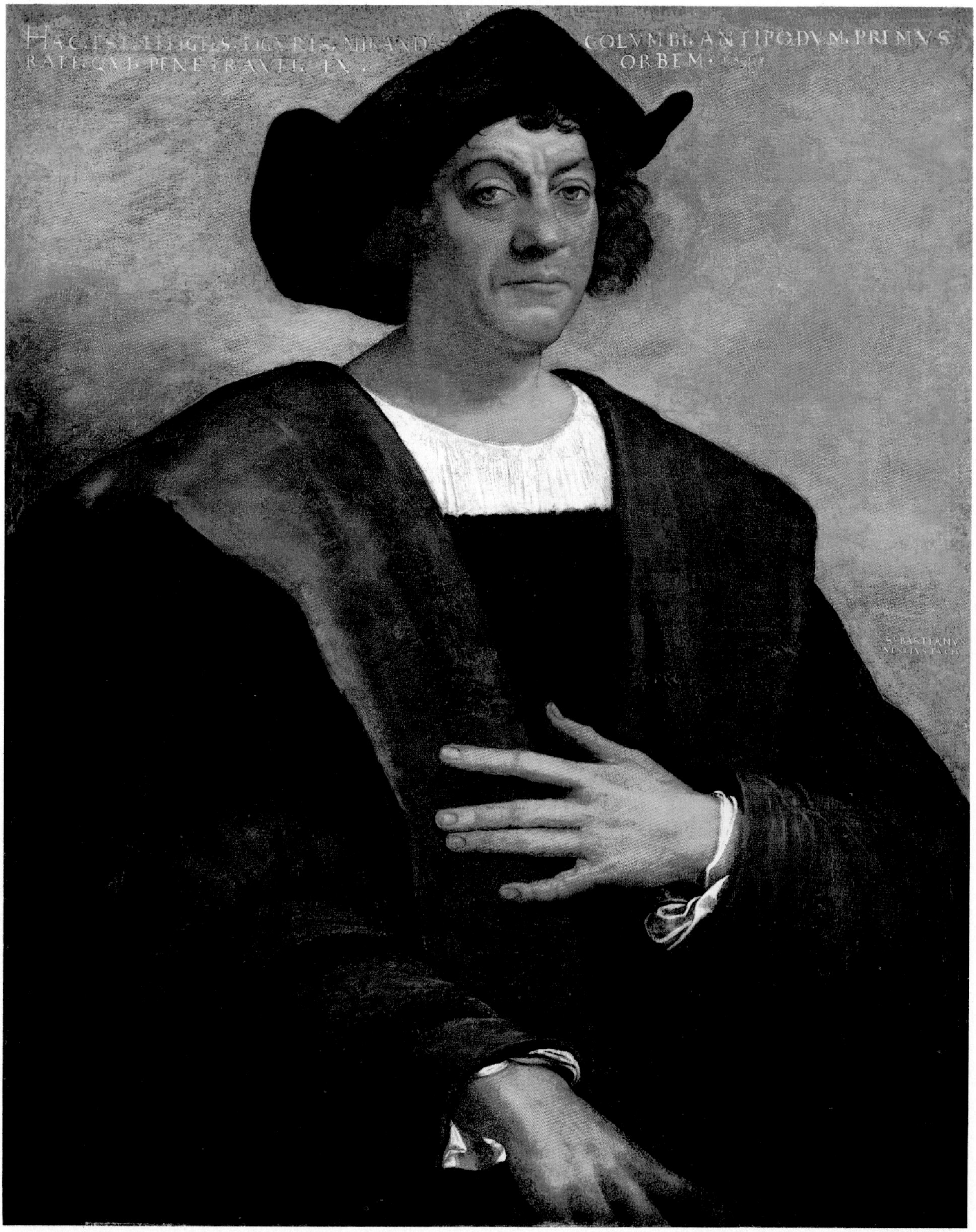
COLVMBI ANTIPODVM PRIMVS
ORBEM

No pictures of Columbus's vessels are known to exist, but these sixteenth-century Portuguese carracks—though much larger than the Santa Maria—are of a very similar type.

you would most likely drop off the earth into some unimaginable, reeling fate. The Portuguese had the best merchant marine of their time, but it took them seventy-five years to map the coastline of West Africa; they hugged the coastline, wriggling cautiously around all its bays and indentations, not caring to go too far beyond sight of land into the Atlantic, which they called the Sea of Gloom.

Geographers and mathematicians were beginning to agree that the earth was round, but there were not too many sailors who cared to believe it. There was, however, a superb one, who had spent much time with astronomers and mathematicians and had been a master mariner with the Portuguese. He was born to a working-class family in Genoa: Cristoforo Colombo, known to his future patrons, the Spanish, as Cristóbal Colón and to us as Christopher Columbus. A giant of a redhead, six feet tall at a time when the average virile male was about five foot four, he was also a fast-talking, obsessive egomaniac who combined in curiosity, romantic stubbornness, and sense of mission something of Galileo, Don Quixote, and John the Baptist. With his brother he had run a profitable map-making firm, but not profitable enough to enable him to launch his grand design: to outflank the infidel Turk by sailing west across the so-called Ocean Sea to reach the spices of the Indies. For, if indeed the world was a sphere, then by sailing west from Europe you would come to the Indies and in time to the farthest reach of the earth's mass, to China and then Japan, or to Japan and then to China. Nobody could say for sure which came first.

The theory that you could reach the Orient by sailing west had been mooted since Roman times. But it was one thing to talk about it and another to dare to prove it. Leonardo da Vinci had made drawings of airplanes several centuries before the Wright brothers, yet making sketches of an attractive fantasy is not the same as getting sponsors for an actual launch. But Columbus, fired by a majestic vision, was prepared to do more than simply prove that the earth was round. A Christian of almost maniacal devoutness, he also longed for the secular trappings of pomp and power, and, beginning with the Indies, he would convert every prince and pauper he encountered and have himself proclaimed governor of every land and island he discovered.

In the late 1470s he began to tramp round Europe, looking for a royal sponsor. And in the following ten years he found none. He was turned down by the King of Portugal; his brother had no better success with the kings of France and England. Three times Columbus watched and waited while King Ferdinand and Queen Isabella of Spain passed his proposals on to royal councils. They called in expert witnesses and three times concluded that the adventure was perilously impractical and ruinously expensive. He was finally led to say that "everyone to whom I spoke of this enterprise thought it a mere jest."

But what must have been the sharpest hurt was the skepticism of the Portuguese. The testimony of their ship builders, navigators, and ships' captains must have been as damning as it was conclusive. They could not, or would not, answer the question of where Africa gave out, whether there could be an alternative route to Asia other than by the north. Most· daunting of all was the mystery of the Atlantic, the visible part of the Ocean Sea itself. No one had any idea how wide it was or what really lay on the other side of it, except quite possibly perdition. Did the islands that whimsically dotted the maps of the Sea really exist? Were they supplied with grain and fruits for reprovisioning? Had they harbors for safe shelter?

Columbus had convinced himself, by calculations both shrewd and wishful, that he had the answer to all these vexatious questions. And the oftener his plan was rejected, the more dogmatic he became. Like many another evangelist, he compensated for public ridicule by growing paranoid. By now he had inflated his original request for a mere expense account into a set of extraordinary demands. He must be entitled Admiral of the Ocean Sea. He must have ten percent of all the treasure, the gold, the loot he scooped up along the way. The governorship of the Indies and of every country and island he discovered must pass through his eldest son to his heirs "for evermore."

It was too much for Ferdinand and Isabella. They said no once again. So early in January 1492 he left Granada, in disgust, "for evermore" and headed north for another appeal to France. But, on the plea of the Queen's confessor, one Juan Pérez (an unsung hero of American history), he was stopped on a bridge at Pinos, six miles north of Granada, and brought back: the Queen was disposed to change her mind.

For one thing, the seven hundred-year-old civil war with the Moors had at last come to an end, for in that same January Granada, the last Islamic stronghold, surrendered. For another, Ferdinand and Isabella were reminded that another Genoese, Giovanni Caboto (whom we know as John Cabot), had convinced Henry VII of England that the Spice Islands could be reached by sea. Thirdly, the court treasurer pointed out to the Queen that Columbus's expedition would cost no more than a couple of royal banquets. And since, like every other European monarch, Isabella was pinched for money after the Turks had cut off trade with the East, and was appalled, like the rest of Christian Europe, by the enormous inroads the Turks were making right on down into Africa, two urgent questions presented themselves, profane and sacred: Who could replenish the royal treasury? And who could save the world for Christ?

In his final eloquent plea, Columbus avowed that both answers could be found in a book recently printed for the first time, the *Travels* of Marco Polo in China, undertaken two centuries before. Columbus had read it, believed it absolutely, and in the year it appeared had started his trek for a sponsor. But now he recited its tempting revelations. The Orient, Marco Polo had written, was a land dripping with spices and paved with gold. And, more miraculous still, it was ruled over by a great Christian prince. If he could be reached, this prince would muster his legions and, allied with the glorious Christian monarchs of a united Spain, would surround and contain the infidel Turk.

Columbus reinforced the testimony of Marco Polo by solemnly recounting the long and ardent conversations he himself had held with the Almighty that confirmed these marvelous revelations. (As his contract was to testify, his visions did not cloud his instinct for ten percent.) His Christian argument prevailed. His contract, all its grandiloquent provisions indulged, was signed at Granada, and, with the royal blessing and a letter to be delivered to the Grand Khan of China (Cathay), he was commissioned to prepare for his expedition "for gospel and for gold."

There was a wrangling interval with the ship builders, who must have felt like an airplane manufacturer of the First World War being asked to raise the money to put John Glenn into space. They were not disposed to build ships that might sail off the edge of the earth. However, they bowed before a command from the Queen, and the royal treasurer underwrote the cost. Columbus needed three ships, but only two had to be built. The third, already in port, was owned by Juan de la Cosa, the man who eight years later was to draw the first map of the New World. It was bought for Columbus and became his flagship, the *Santa María*. Today it would not be acceptable as a Riviera yacht.

Only one hundred tons in weight and seventy-five feet long, the *Santa María* was not by a long shot one of the big ships of the time, but it was what was needed—a tough maneuverable tub, something between a freighter and a PT boat, sturdy enough to withstand roaring storms and agile enough to take quick shelter in the shallow channels of the imagined Atlantic islands. It was smeared with pitch against barnacles and had stones for ballast. It had a mainmast as long as the keel, one huge square sail, and a small topsail. The two accompanying ships, the *Pinta* and the *Niña,* were made over into square-riggers. They were all equipped with a gun or two against the unlikely risk of pirates, and among the more interesting provisions was red wine, the standard laxative, but to the amount of two and a half liters per man per day—which sounds like a very generous ration, though it could well have been meant to keep them all philosophical if the worst happened.

There were forty men—one Portuguese, another Italian, and the rest all Spaniards—aboard the flotilla, including a surgeon and the royal controller of accounts, sent along to keep tabs on Columbus's swindle sheet when he started to figure the cost of the gold and the spices he would accumulate. There was also a converted Jew who spoke Arabic, which was thought to be very similar to Chinese; he would be the interpreter. On the evening of August 2, 1492, the entire crew went ashore for confession, and on the next morning they set sail from Palos.

They sailed through August and September and came on none of those islands with which geographers had fancifully dotted the Atlantic. The crews grew weary, then anxious, then panicky. After a bout with the trade winds, which would slam at them on the homeward journey, they were close to mutiny. The captains of the two other ships at last signaled for a rendezvous and begged Columbus to turn back. He did his subtle best to reassure them by showing them the log, which he had faked to reduce the record of the miles they had gone from Spain. However, he must have had appalling apprehensions of his own, for he had miscalculated the width of the Sea of Gloom by about fifty percent.

He promised the captains that, if they were still in open sea forty-eight hours later, he would turn back. On the night of October 11, he swears, he "prayed mightily to the Lord." Whether by luck or divine intervention, on the following day he sighted, as he believed, the mainland of Asia or one of its offshore islands. We know it as San Salvador in the Bahamas. He went on to explore Haiti and then Cuba, which he soon decided was Marco Polo's Zipangu (Japan). He was a little puzzled by the absence of cities, but there *were* spices, and cotton, and weird birds, and coppery-colored natives, who kept assuring him—as the Indians did to all succeeding explorers—that inland, always farther inland, there were mountains of gold.

Till his dying day, Columbus never knew that he had not touched the Orient. For the present he was jubilantly convinced that he had, and like a good salesman he hurried back to Spain with what we should call display samples of the products of Japan: exotic plants, brilliant parrots, an alligator, prize natives got up like show horses, a little gold. His foreign sales exhibition was a brilliant success. For his second voyage he fitted out a fleet of seventeen ships, and there was a rush of fifteen hundred men—sailors, soldiers, youngsters on the loose—to explore the wonders of Asia, as well as a clutch of priests to sanctify the expedition and convert the potential slaves.

When Columbus landed again he paused only long enough to deplore the fact that the men he had left behind, having grabbed everything in sight including the native girls, had been massacred. He pushed on into Haiti, and here, in the stream beds, he did find considerable gold. He traced the coast of Cuba until it turned southwest and convinced himself he was now in southern China.

Once more he went home, taking with him this time the contractual five percent of the royal ration of gold. In spite of an oath of secrecy given to the controller of accounts, the magic word "gold" leaked out and very soon there was a more desperate rush of eager adventurers—"not a man," it was written, "down to the very tailors who does not beg to be allowed to become a discoverer." Now began the longest, most determined, and most brutal gold rush in history.

For centuries the Spanish have borne, with considerable ire, the weight of this shameful story. And perhaps we ought to throw in here the reminder that if the Spanish of the late fifteenth and early sixteenth centuries combined great physical courage, endurance, and intense religious zeal with devastating cruelty, they probably behaved no worse than any other Europeans would have done who got there first. British schoolbooks confidently describe the English sea dogs Drake and Hawkins as honest, dauntless men. But Drake's brutalities in sacking the cities of the west coast of South America are a byword among the learned, and Hawkins had spent many untroubled years in the Spanish slave trade. Yet we cannot ignore the exhaustive records of how the Spanish went on the rampage through Central America and Mexico exhausting whole populations in the mines, so that an honest sergeant recalling the cruelties of his life in Mexico lamented that "there was more gold than health." The marching orders prescribed a ruthless routine: round up the natives, prohibit their religion, enslave them, exhaust the gold, and move on—to more gold, silver, pearls. "Everything," wrote a chronicler, "at the Equator is rich."

As the later Cortés pushed inland, he came on cities with temples, pyramids, lighthouses, aqueducts, poets, and philosophers. The range and the customs of the native cultures were bewildering, to say the least, and less susceptible to roughshod suppression. So a simple murderous catechism was applied. After Columbus's first voyage, the Pope, a Spaniard, had drawn a line one hundred leagues west of the Azores and decreed that "everything beyond that which shall be charted by our beloved servants shall belong to Spain," as a part of Christendom. (After a thundering protest from the Portuguese, they too were included, as "our brothers," in the new dominion.) The King of Spain had proclaimed his title to it as New Spain. If, therefore, a kingdom or a tribe was hostile, it was no more than a Christian duty to suppress it, to topple its idols, and raise the Cross on the grounds that the natives were double traitors: to the Pope of Rome and the King of Spain, two deities of whom they had never heard.

If the natives were merely sulky or obstinate, they were terrified into submission by two horrors they had never encountered: the firing of monster machines called cannon, and the appearance of living monsters

Most Indian artifacts were stripped of their gold by Spanish conquistadors. But this brilliant headdress, formed of feathers and encrusted with pure gold, somehow survived.

35

cities, its temple walls draped inside and out with precious stones, the "very wealthy" inhabitants wearing girdles of gold and riding on camels and elephants. It could be, it had to be, the delirious friar decided, the road to Cathay.

The written report of Fray Marcos thrilled Mexico City and Madrid and made him for a year or two the most famous man in New and Old Spain. Mendoza at once made Coronado captain-general of a land expedition to retrace the friar's journey and annex the cities of gold. In February 1540 Coronado, in gilded armor, set out from Compostela with two hundred and fifty horsemen, seventy Spanish foot soldiers, a thousand reliable (that is to say, tamed or friendly) Indians, baggage animals, sheep, goats, herds of cattle, and a train of priests.

Within the month Coronado had entered Culiacán, halfway up the mainland coast of the Gulf of California, which was then the northernmost outpost of New Spain. For another month he followed the river streams and continued with a tough advance party up into the mountains. Once through them on the eastern slopes, he saw ahead of him an unbroken horizon of desert and boulders and scrubland. It was formidable but it was, according to the Marcos report, the route to the Seven Cities. Coronado slogged across it, through Arizona and on into New Mexico, and at the beginning of July, in infernal heat, came into the first of the cities. It was a pueblo of adobe huts, in what has long been the Zuñi Indian country, and after a brief struggle the captain-general took this rude village. There were no camels or elephants or cows, no gold ornaments hanging from trees—indeed, no trees. Nothing but a continuous lunar landscape. Coronado pitched camp to rest and, heavy with disappointment, re-formed his forces and picked scouting parties to go to the east and west and find the glittering prize. The northwestern party was stopped by the apocalyptic deep of the Grand Canyon of the Colorado River. Another party found another collection of seven villages, as rude as the first.

During that first winter Coronado was disheartened enough to seize on the story of an Indian slave that far off to the east there was a rich and populous city known as Quivira. This, then, became the new El Dorado, and, fourteen months after he had started, Coronado marched on into Texas and then, encouraged by other native rumors, turned north again and on through Kansas. They came at last to Quivira, way to the north of our Dodge City. It was yet another miserable village, of the Wichita tribe. In a final venture, he sent out other scouting parties, and they returned and told the same story—rolling, inhospitable plains, small primitive villages. So at last he went back to the main body of his army, which had been limping along well behind the advance guard. We tear through this country today on paved divided highways, and it is impossible for us now to realize not only the arduousness of Coronado's march but the daily afflictions they took for granted. Most of his horsemen and foot soldiers wore about thirty pounds of armor. They rarely found a stream or lake to bathe in, and hemorrhoids and fistulas were as common as the common cold. Inevitably, the doctors they took along were surgeons.

Coronado had in two years gone up the Gulf of California, through Arizona and New Mexico and Texas, and wheeled into northern Kansas to the Nebraska border before he gave up. In the spring of 1542 he turned south again, marched down by a shorter route along the line of the Santa Fe Trail to the Rio Grande and then westward through the Zuñi country and wretched Cíbola, then through the mountain passages again and down the Gulf of California to Mexico City. He and his troop arrived there in the autumn, full of thought, empty of any riches, "very sad and very weary, completely worn out and shamefaced."

There are very few traces of this epic though shattering march. There is one, an immense mesa crowned by an Indian pueblo brooding over the boulder-strewn desert below. It is Acoma, in New Mexico, about forty miles west of Albuquerque. One of Coronado's scouts saw it and returned to the main camp to tell of "a great city in the sky . . . the strongest position ever seen in the world." Coronado decided to give it a miss—and wisely, for it was the stronghold of a hostile tribe that remained unconquered by the Spanish for fifty-nine years after Coronado's men saw it. Indeed, the Ácomas live on the crest there today as they have lived for over a thousand years.

Ácoma is the site of one of the last and most ferocious onslaughts the Spanish were to make, in defiance of the Pope's proclamation about the humanity of the Indian. The three-day and -night assault is celebrated in an epic poem, and certainly the Spanish took an epic revenge for the Ácomas' half century of resistance, killing six hundred and imprisoning as many, tossing the seventy warrior chieftains off the great cliff and binding to lifetime servitude another five hundred, mostly women and children. Those who could not be wooed out of their religion were literally thrown to the dogs or flogged into devotion to the Carpenter of Nazareth.

But, as usual, time softened the sting of these atrocities, and thirty years later a mild Franciscan priest, Father Ramírez, walked to the fortress barefoot and unarmed and, with the single weapon of a cross, converted the Ácomas.

There is also, another twenty miles to the west, a towering bluff, El

Overleaf: *Three hundred and fifty feet above the desert floor, the still-occupied adobe buildings of Ácoma perch on the edge of their red sandstone mesa.*

Morro. Indian guides led Coronado to it when his men were fainting from thirst. At its foot is a pool of pure water, and on its massive face, smoothed by the desert winds to the sheen of bones, is an inscription in Spanish done with the point of a sword by a grandee who came along sixty-odd years later to find, from Coronado's map, the same oasis. It says: "Through here passed the Governor Don Juan de Oñate, after his discovery of the Sea of the South, 16 April 1605." (By the Sea of the South he meant that he had been as far as the Gulf of California.) This Oñate set up the first Spanish government in the Southwest, and it is worth a passing thought—from an Englishman, anyway—that the Palace of the Governors at Santa Fe was built ten years before the Pilgrims landed on the Massachusetts coast.

But, even by Oñate's time the dream of extending New Spain through North America had been shattered once for all—and not in America or by its natives, but by the greatest sea battle of the sixteenth century. Philip of Spain's free access to North America depended, like Napoleon's or Hitler's, on mastering Europe by the conquest of Britain. And when, in the summer of 1588, the "invincible" Armada was first battered by the broadsides of the English sea dogs, then panicked by fire ships, and then scattered by a shift of the wind as far north as the Firth of Forth, Spain's grip on New Spain was frozen where it had first taken hold. The Atlantic thereafter became an open highway for the Dutch, the French, and most of all the English; and from then on Spain was powerless to prevent the planting in turn of New France in Canada and a new England in Virginia and Massachusetts.

For the next two hundred years these remote provinces of New Spain—today's Arizona, Texas, California, and New Mexico—slowly developed an outpost economy and a military government throughout a burning landscape half the size of Europe. The Spanish had introduced the two indispensable elements of life in western America, the horse and the cow. It was the horse that first terrified the Indian into submission; it was the horse that set him free, and freewheeling, from Mexico to the Canadian tundra.

The Spanish also left behind, in their branding signs and the embossing of saddles, a whole heraldry of ranching, and in conjunction with this they established the rodeo. The purpose of the rodeo was to round up, once a year, all the cattle that had run free or multiplied on the open range; to distinguish one man's herd from another, the yearling calves were branded with the owner's initials or some chosen emblems registered with the governor of each province. While the word "cowboy" is a direct translation of *vaquero*, much of the language of ranching, and the Spanish words for the kind of country it was done in, have passed over to the present-day practitioners and, indeed, to most children brought up in the Southwest: corral, mesa, arroyo, patio, adobe, mustang, sombrero, desperado, poncho, alfalfa, bronco. By small changes or abbreviation, other Spanish words were naturalized in English: "stampede" for *estampida*, "lariat" for *(la) reata*, "lasso" for *lazo*, "chaps" for *chaperajos*, which protected the wearer against the desert scrub called "chaparral" *(chaparro)*. The word "cinch," until fairly recently a common slang word for something quickly or easily done, derives from the Spanish word for the saddle girth, *cincha*. When it was securely fastened, it was said to be "cinched."

During the eighteenth century, the plundering life of the conquistadors gave way to the vigorous life of the *rancheros*. The last great military expedition came about through one of those paranoid rumors from which even the most civilized nations are not exempt. In the late 1760s Upper California—what we today call California—was part of New Spain, though it had been only vaguely explored, not settled. The only people known to live there were Indians rumored to be so fierce that the captain-general who had conquered all of Lower California said that to subdue them it would be necessary to hire sixty gorillas from Guatemala. The Spanish governors, secure down in Mexico, had no plans to colonize the north, until King Charles III of Spain received a report that Russians had been sighted in Monterey Bay in alarming numbers. They were heralds of a nightmare that has haunted California into our own time: the Russian menace. The Russians had been drawn there by the presence, in large schools, of the sea otter, which brought fantastic prices in the China trade. The skins could be exchanged for quicksilver, the absence of which in California had hampered the development of the provinces of New Spain; for at that time quicksilver (mercury) was the magic element for extracting gold and silver from their ores. But it was dreadfully obvious to the King of Spain that the Russians were intending to set up an empire in Upper California. In simple fact, the Russians wanted nothing more than the sea otter himself, a plump and comical beast, a Disney version of Colonel Blimp, who has the round brown face of a well-fed cat and swims on his back, his belly protruding, his whiskers bristling, his paws calmly folded across his chest. Indeed, when the sea otter was fished out, the Russians left.

But long before then King Charles had ordered military expeditions out of Mexico by land and sea, to build a chain of forts and hold the coast of California. As always, priests went along to lend a degree of humanity to the job of "pacifying" the natives. For this special mission, a Franciscan, Father Junípero Serra, was sent out to Mexico in 1767 and a year later started off with Captain Gaspar de Portolá on the conquering land expedition into Alta (Upper) California. If in the Spanish record there is one man more than another whose life could possibly redeem the

ferocity of the conquistadors, Father Serra is that man. He gave himself wholly to the barbaric Indians, and, for every fort built to protect the coastline he built a mission, so that the Russian menace bore some fruit in producing the twenty-one missions that are the Spaniards' main architectural legacy to California.

Altogether, Father Serra walked between four and five thousand miles up and down the coastline and the inland valleys on an infected foot he refused to treat, over scrub desert and through dense mountains, always stopping on saints' days to lay the foundations of a mission and ring a bell and cry, "Come, come and receive the faith of Christ." The route of his walk is today the route of the main north-south highway, and it is vividly marked in the spring by the blossoming mustard whose seeds the friar scattered as he went. Father Serra, who died in his seventieth year at Carmel, is the first and noblest of a great, though not greatly prized, American tradition: the priests, in the main Spanish and then French, who crossed the seas and tramped the enormous curve of wilderness from Lower California around to Montana to care for a few Indians and, later, trappers. Junípero Serra, De Smet, Ravalli, Megarini, Prando, Father Point. They accepted the terrible emptiness of the West as the good ground to work in, carried the barest essentials and lived out their Catholicism in the fearful innocence of its Founder.

Apart from the thousands of Spanish place names, the march across the American landscape from the eastern border of Texas, through the Southwest and up and along the nine hundred-mile sweep of today's California, there are one or two other relics of the Spanish empire in North America that ought to be mentioned, for I doubt that one American in a hundred is aware that they are part of the Spanish legacy. I refer to several of the basic American crops—oats, wheat, barley, and oranges. And it was the Spanish who took the rudest indigenous cereal of the Indians and made it the sustaining staple from the Canadian border to Cape Horn—namely, maize, everywhere in America called "corn," in accordance with the habit of all English-speaking countries in giving the name to their commonest staple crop, whether it is oats, barley, or—as in England—wheat. (When the Americans introduced the dry breakfast cereal to Britain, they had the tact not to market cornflakes in translation as "maize flakes"; had they done so, it is pretty certain that the custom would not have caught on.)

Of the other nations that explored the New World and were to challenge England for a claim to it—most notably the Netherlands, Portugal, and

By the late eighteenth century, the Spanish had created a stable, easy society in California, with estates built near such missions as San Carlos de Borromeo.

France—much the most impressive was France. She was also the first. If it comes as a surprise to hear that Spain had set up the first government in the West in Santa Fe eleven years before the Pilgrims stumbled on Cape Cod, a bigger surprise is available in the news that the French started their colonial experiment in North America a hundred years before the *Mayflower.*

Only twelve years after Columbus's first voyage, Breton fishermen started to work the cod banks off Nova Scotia. And, while the Portuguese and the English were ferreting along the North American coast from Labrador to Florida, trying to find the entrance to that waterway through to the Orient, the humble Bretons were pushing into the mainland and coming on Indians loaded with animal furs. Although the Bretons found to their delight that they could catch fish in those waters simply by hauling them up in baskets, they soon began to see the possibilities of a profitable fur trade. The Indians were as fascinated by bits of metal, axes, and iron kettles as the Bretons were by the furs.

This simple system of barter was the start of a fur trade that burgeoned when the fishermen penetrated the gulf and the river of Saint Lawrence. In time they abandoned the cod for the beaver and were soon trapping and skinning every animal in sight—and, incidentally, putting out the tentacles of the French dominion in the North. An empire could not, of course, be built and held by a scattered army of trappers and fishermen, however hardy. But in their way these simple Bretons were the poor man's conquistadors of the North. Their descendants helped form a new nation, reaching from the Atlantic to the Pacific, and they still live there securely nearly a century after Spain lost every big and little holding in the New World.

The French "kingdoms in the North" were made possible by four explorers—Verrazano, Cartier, Champlain, and La Salle—and, in the first place by a King of France who had the nerve to snap his fingers at the Pope. Francis I was born two years after Columbus landed at San Salvador and came to the throne when he was twenty-one. A violent athlete, with a passion for hunting, tennis, and women, by the time he reached his late twenties he needed all the revenues he could lay his hands on to satisfy the luxury of his court and the foibles of his mistresses. By then the French, the English, the Irish, and the Dutch had begun the systematic piracy of Spanish ships homeward bound with the loot of "the Indies." In 1522 Cortés celebrated the final conquest of Mexico by packing into a galleon a curator's collection of gold and silver objects and mosaic masks. The shipment was captured by the French on the last leg of its journey, off the tip of Portugal at Cape Saint Vincent. It exhibited in dazzling fashion the wealth of the Indies and egged on the fond suspicion of Francis I that perhaps a shorter route to similar treasure lay through the Far North of America. Francis was a blundering and profligate ruler but he has immortalized himself, in the history of America, by his sharp retort to a furious reminder from Spain that the Pope had proclaimed everything a hundred leagues west of the Azores as Spanish property: "We fail to find this clause in Adam's will."

Francis decided it was France's turn to discover the northern passage to the Indies. He chose his own Columbus in another Genoese, Giovanni da Verrazano, got the money for an expedition from the French silk merchants, and sent Verrazano off. Verrazano had no luck finding the elusive passage in the West Indies and sailed instead all the way up the North American coast. Chesapeake Bay turned out to be a bay. He paused to decide that the Hudson River was probably another, and he sailed on past Cape Cod, probed the coast of Maine, and continued on to Newfoundland and the Strait of Belle Isle.

This was a letdown, but Francis I did not give up. Ten years later Jacques Cartier, a wealthy citizen of St. Malo and an expert navigator, concentrated on the North and made two voyages there, following and naming the Saint Lawrence. Still no strait, no open way to China. But he found his Fray Marcos in a Huron chief, Donnaconna, who seduced him with tales of a northern Cíbola. It was an inland kingdom called Saguenay. It too was supposed to have mines groaning with gold and silver, to grow fragrant spices, to be populated by men bespangled with rubies who flew like bats. Cartier took Donnaconna back to France to sell this fantasy to the King, who was too excited by its gaudy promise to doubt it, so Cartier returned with his chief. But, just as the Caribs and the natives of Mexico had always promised gold over the next mountain range, Cartier was endlessly assured that Saguenay lay just across the next marsh, the farthest island in a waste of tundra. Like Columbus, Cartier thought he had better return with at least a few samples of the undiscovered mines. He took back quartz crystals.

After these fruitless searches, the French were too busy fighting among themselves to spare any more ships or money for another try, and for another fifty years the discovery of the interior of Canada (an Indian word meaning *pueblo,* or "village") was left to the fur trappers and traders. Instead of governors' mansions, trading posts rose between the present cities of Quebec and Montreal. Meanwhile, the French corsairs knew enough about the Bahama Channel and the Florida coast to be encouraged to try founding a colony in Florida. But they were beaten and pretty well annihilated by the Spanish, who in 1565 built at Saint Augustine the first of a line of forts going up as far as the Carolinas in order to protect their homebound ships from the pestiferous French pirates.

This unadventurous half century could well have marked the beginning of the end of French ambitions in North America, had it not been

In the manuscript of one of his New World journals, the great French explorer Samuel Champlain left this gory drawing — a group of presumably heathen Indians expiating their sins at the hands of two Spanish Inquisitors in Mexico. The French prided themselves on having much better relations with the Indians in their own territories of New France.

for the prosperous growth of the fur trade. Toward the end of the sixteenth century, it occurred—and to other Europeans as well as the French—that furs were a more tangible asset than rumors of gold. The summer haul along the Saint Lawrence was enormous, and France decided it was time to organize and monopolize it. And yet the belief in that sea passage through North America was so tenacious, so tantalizing to navigators and geographers and greedy monarchs, that the conquest of the fur trade and the establishment of New France were mere by-products of it.

Samuel Champlain was a sailor, a soldier, and a fanatical geographer who, in spite of the vague contemporary notions of longitude, loved to speculate about the width of America and draw imaginary maps of the whole continent, in one of them hinting at the existence of a Panama canal. After a two-year voyage to the West Indies, he was sent, in 1603, out to Canada, ostensibly to advance the business of a man who had been given a monopoly of the fur trade by King Henry IV, actually to map for the first time the convolutions and geographical relation of the Saint Lawrence, Saguenay, Ottawa, and Richelieu rivers. He was to trace their courses, note the prospects for farming and settlement of the lands they traversed—and, as a sideline and serious hobby, to see if any of these rivers flowed from the legendary inland sea.

Champlain was the first man to see that this vast expanse of marshland, plain, rivers, lily pads, and semi-tundra, and the many Indian tribes who inhabited it, could be made into a large self-sustaining colony only by Frenchmen who would come to America for keeps, learn about the new land, bargain and work with the natives, and settle. He set the example by founding Quebec as a base and from there investigating Lakes Huron and Ontario—and, by siding with the friendly Algonquins and Hurons, defeating the Iroquois, whom he rightly took to be the tribe most hostile to a white foothold. For the rest of his life, through the loss and renewal of trade monopolies, he was as busy as the beaver he sought to capture in fair dealing with the Indians who caught it. John Bartlet Brebner saw in him a true exemplar:

> Nothing is more notable in the conduct of the French in North America than their success in getting along with the Indians and in living among them. It was Champlain who invented, as it were, the *coureurs du bois* [the fur traders in the woods] and the *voyageurs* [the traders on the plains] who carried French influence from the St. Lawrence to the Rockies and from Hudson Bay to the Gulf of Mexico.

The last phrase suggests a leap of French ambition far beyond the northern wilderness. And this brings us, by a comparable leap in time, to the French Coronado, Sieur de La Salle. The interval between the virtual settlement of Quebec and the appearance in Canada of La Salle, a twenty-three-year-old emigrant, is about another sixty years. In that time France became the political and cultural leader of continental Europe, but New France almost expired. In the early years the colony suffered from a politer but no less enervating form of the gang wars that harassed Chicago in the era of Prohibition: ruthless squabbles over whose "territory" belonged to whom among monopolists and merchants who had expected to make a quick million in the now legendary fur trade. But, in the later years, New France had an open and declared enemy in the tribal alliance usually called the Five Nations and known to the French as the Iroquois League. For five years or so the Iroquois—with the help of the Dutch—tried to drive the French traders and hunters into their stockades and to destroy their settlements. A new and, to the Iroquois, obnoxious feature of Canadian life was the horde of Jesuit priests who, in a burst of missionary zeal, had arrived and gone to work on saving the Hurons and the other friendly Indians. Unfortunately they did not regard the Iroquois as beyond redemption, and many of them suffered abominably for their evangelical efforts in the back country. By 1663 the young Louis XIV had responded to frantic appeals from the besieged settlements and sent out an army of men, weapons, money, and colonists, and one able administrator, to stabilize the colony and convert it into a royal province. But the Iroquois guerrillas remained unbeatable.

In the summer of 1665 there arrived, in the person of the Marquis de Tracy, a first-rate soldier to dispose of them with almost Spanish ferocity, in a campaign of "total warfare" that has come to seem intolerably inhumane only in the last decade or so: to defeat not merely the enemy's armies but to ruin his supplies, burn his villages, and cripple the life of the noncombatants. Tracy waited until the crops of the Mohawk Valley were ripe and then descended, with eight hundred veterans of wars with the Turks. He crushed the tribes, burned the fields and villages, destroyed the stores, and broke once for all the threat of the Iroquois. Half of his men found the prospects of Canada promising enough to stay for life.

The defeat of the Iroquois was timely; La Salle came along to Montreal a year later to go into the fur trade, and had they still been on the warpath they would doubtless have denied him the glory of his historic voyage through the hinterland of America down to the Gulf of Mexico.

Like so many heroes, villains, and ordinaries of the seventeenth and eighteenth centuries, La Salle is a hard man to fix as a recognizable human type. The contemporary store of abstract virtues and vices has let loose on him a shower of adjectives that still fail to pin him down. He is described as audacious, diplomatic, overbearing, brilliant, courageous, a man of "inexhaustible pride," "inflexible purposes," and "insatiable intellect," all of which sounds very impressive but still leaves the picture of a

faceless demigod. We can only try to snatch a hint of his mettle, his uniqueness as an undefeatable explorer, by tracing briefly the route of his enormous trip.

He prepared himself for it by learning a dozen Indian dialects and determining at all costs to make the Indians along the way his friends. He went back to France to get the money for enlarging the fur trade through to the rolling plains of the West, which had discouraged Cartier. He no doubt mentioned the usual aim of finding a passage through to the Orient, but he evidently took a dry Gallic view of it, for he named the rapids on the Saint Lawrence seigneury he had been granted—Lachine. His main aim was toward a French empire designed to conquer the hinterland of America and to keep the English, by now well planted in Virginia and New England, shut in east of the Appalachians.

There were several reconnaissance trips into the wilderness below Lakes Ontario and Erie. The last one, launched in November 1679, was that of the *Griffin*, the first ship to sail on Lake Erie. It went to Green Bay, Wisconsin, and loaded up with furs, with which La Salle hoped to placate his backers in Montreal, and it was never heard of again. La Salle, quite unaware of this disaster, went on around the west shore of Lake Michigan, built a fort at the mouth of the Saint Joseph River, portaged to the Illinois, built another fort to protect a tribe of friendly Indians, and then paused for the grand slide down the Mississippi. But by now he needed more supplies, and, having heard of the disaster to the *Griffin*, he raced—and "raced" is not too flip a word to describe a canoe-and-carry trip of a thousand miles in sixty-five days—back to Fort Frontenac, at Kingston, Ontario, to talk his jaundiced backers into providing more funds.

The next winter he did the whole trip back again by canoe and foot, only to find that the latest fort had been abandoned and his men had deserted. So he walked and canoed the thousand miles back again to Frontenac. This indestructible optimist got some more money and supplies and once more trekked the thousand miles back to the Saint Joseph fort. From there, leading twenty-three Frenchmen and thirty-one Indians, he started the long last lap down the continent's central watershed.

It was December 1681, and the rivers were frozen—a mere nuisance to La Salle, who had nearly starved in appalling weather on his first approach to the Illinois River. He made sledges for the canoes and the men pulled them across the Chicago River and down the Illinois, usually wearing out a pair of leather moccasins a day. They came at last to

This detail of Indians and a beached canoe is from a picture painted near Quebec in the eighteenth century by an amateur artist.

running water, and early in February floated into the Mississippi. The snow banks melted, the downriver current quickened, the early semi-tropical spring came in, high tides swirled around the fronds of live oaks against the shore, and the happy party paddled easily down the thousand miles and more of the great river and came to its mouth. There they divided into three groups, and each took a separate channel to the Passes, where the Mississippi debouches into the Gulf. Three days later, on April 9, 1682, they stood together on a small bluff overlooking the sea. La Salle raised a cross and planted the banner of France and annexed "this country of Louisiana," named at that moment after "the most high, mighty, invincible and victorious Louis the Great, by Grace of God, King of France and Navarre."

La Salle claimed nothing less than the whole Mississippi watershed. He then made the huge journey back to Quebec, pardonably proud in the knowledge that he had made friends and allies of all the Indian tribes he had come across and, by deliberately so doing, had fortified the claim of "Louis the Great" with the best kind of allies an empire builder can have, the natives on their own ground. But what he faced in Quebec was a new governor who loathed him and belittled his great expedition. Without money and without favor, he sailed home for France to make a personal appeal to the King to finance his planting of the southern capital of the new empire on the spot where he had raised the King's banner. Louis, who had been maliciously primed by the new governor, told La Salle that his voyage of discovery had been a vast waste of time, but ultimately thinking to twist a knife in the back of his chief enemy, the King of Spain, he relented and equipped La Salle with four ships, soldiers, and colonists of both sexes to build his fort on the Gulf and "control the continent."

La Salle sailed in 1684, and it ought to have been a triumphant return. But this last sorry chapter took nearly three years. La Salle, a tragic victim of the contemporary ignorance about longitude, overshot the Passes by four hundred miles, landed on the Texas coast, and began a march as forlorn as Coronado's—not to find a city of gold but merely to find again the majestic river whose length he had traversed! Nobody knows how many thousand miles his colonizers walked or in how many directions. They lived off the bison and the corn of Indians who were as vague about the Mississippi as they were about the Seine. La Salle, who had started with over four hundred men, by the spring of 1687 was down to forty-five—many dead, others having deserted. Two of his ships had been wrecked and a third gone back to France. In the last ship he took sail again, as he hoped, for Canada, got lost and was beaten by storms back into the Gulf.

He made one last try; he took twenty men on foot across a stretch of rolling prairie. Here, where two centuries later German and Polish farmers settled, there is a bronze statue of La Salle looking across to the stores and automobile sales lots of Navasota, Texas. For here, close by the Navasota River, still 350 miles from the Mississippi, La Salle's men could take no more. They murdered him and mooched off, leaving his naked body to the wind and the buzzards.

In time, of course, the French built the port of New Orleans. Yet they never domesticated the great watershed La Salle had claimed. As so often happens, a man aims at the bull's eye, but strikes on the periphery are what he is remembered by. La Salle had gone on his last voyage to France exalted by the vision of a French empire in the Mississippi Valley that would checkmate the ambitions of the English and the Spanish. What he actually accomplished, almost inadvertently, was to build a loose link of forts and bind them with the friendships of many tribes, so that when the time came, nearly a century after him, the French would be in a position to challenge the English conquest of the continent.

A French map of America of 1765 shows what an exclusive hold they had in the north, even though they were almost as vague about what lay to the south and west as the Spanish had been about what lay to their north and west. Being trappers and rivermen, the French did an incomparable job of mapping the entire nervous system of the rivers, but at any distance to the west of them they simply put in the names of Indian tribes—the Miamis, the Illinois, the Sioux. After La Salle they did not plant colonies on the English model—that is to say, thriving, static, self-governing settlements. They settled always close to the rivers, especially to "the Father of Waters," in way stations, or what we should call retail centers, for the downriver traffic bearing fur and hides and timber to the port of New Orleans. If they found a useful local product—salt, a mineral—they stopped and made a town. In one such, St. Genevieve, Missouri, they made a little Paris, planting their familiar vines and gardens, inviting remote French families with aspirations to gentility to send their children for the purpose of learning good French and attending a school of manners where they might acquire "the two elements of true politeness—grace and self-denial."

It must be obvious by now that Spain's imperial ambitions were arrested too soon for her to build, as the French did, in New Orleans, a full-blown capital city, which might well have been the capital of the United States if Napoleon had not sold for cash the huge interior that La Salle had claimed as Louisiana. But the French—and subsequently the Spanish—prospered there and for the better part of a century it was an overseas metropolis of an easygoing Latin type, where lawyers, bankers,

LE COMMERC

A hopeful promotion piece
published by the French
Mississippi Company in
1717 showed Indians
trading gold and silver
for cheap European goods
at a nonexistent "Port of
Mississippi." The follow-
ing year, the town of New
Orleans was laid out.

QUE LES INDIENS DU MEXIQUE FONT AVEC LES FRANCOIS AU PORT DE MISSISIPI.

merchants, shippers, diplomats, and playboys maintained their quadroon mistresses in the terraced apartments of the Vieux Carré. But though the French Quarter of New Orleans retains—where it does not try too hard—some of the flavor of late eighteenth- and early nineteenth-century France, you will not find there many reminders of the great Frenchmen who created the towns of the Great Lakes and the Mississippi Valley. Only linguistic scholars are aware that the state of Arkansas is still pronounced Arkansaw because that's the way the French pronounced it. (The Arkansas River rises in country settled by Yankees and Germans and is consequently pronounced the way it's spelled.) The same is true of Chicago, which an Englishman has to learn is Shicago, not Tchicago.

Yet the French legacy to all of North America is incalculable and far-ranging. You have only to glance at the map, westward from Quebec twelve hundred miles to Duluth (named for Sieur Du Lhut), and then follow the names of the river towns down to Baton Rouge and New Orleans, to see how many places that we take for granted as Yankee establishments were founded by the French. There are many other places whose origin is not so obvious because of the gift of later settlers for fracturing the French names. Marietta, Ohio, was named after Marie Antoinette, and Narbonne turned into Jawbone. And an Irish railroad gang, coming on a lake in Arkansas that the French had named L'Eau Froid, struggled awhile and left it on the map as Low Freight.

It is not invidious to say that the French influence was far more benign than that of the Spanish. For one thing, the diligence of Huguenots who had been persecuted at home guaranteed not only their decent treatment in the new country but an actual compact with the Catholic Church that both religions would live "in all Christian harmony." There remain, of course, Catholic churches all the way down the Mississippi watershed. But the practical domination of the Church declined very rapidly after France lost her territory west of the Mississippi at the end of the French and Indian Wars. All the upriver French priests were recalled to New Orleans, where today there are more Catholics in a single parish than in most of the Southern states combined. When the priests were finally allowed to return, a missionary bishop found people who had not had the sacraments for forty years.

They had been seduced, he concluded, by the "diabolical writings" of Rousseau, Voltaire, Thomas Paine, and Jefferson. Later on, the sacramental wine was diluted forever in the invading flood of Methodists and Baptists, not to mention the more heathenish "Anglo-American population" deplored by the remaining priests as "infidels of a low and indecent grade."

But the main achievement, which Americans south of the Canadian border forget or never knew, is that the French were the first Western-ers. It is a thousand miles from Quebec to the western shore of Lake Michigan. First, they paddled the waters, then tracked the game on the surrounding lands. Then they organized the commerce of hundreds of tributary rivers and behaved most of the time not as interlopers but as cohabitors of a continent who had much to learn from the original Americans. They developed a breed unknown to the Spanish and the English: the trader-trapper, the water-borne businessman, living rough and mobile, learning from the natives all the vagaries of a new geography—new animals, humans, vegetables, and climate.

In the beginning no four-legged thing was safe from a Frenchman, and in the end no barren prairie, no mountain range was inaccessible to the *voyageurs*. They carried the fur trade two thousand miles inland to the Tetons (ribaldly named, by the way, for the mammary configurations of their peaks). They could live on the barest vegetation and the crudest shelter the plains or the snow-laden Rockies and Sierras could provide. It was French guides who staffed the expedition of Lewis and Clark. And when we trace the routes—especially the cutoffs—that pioneers as late as the gold rushers took, we come on names like Sublette and La Bonté, for, in terrifying places where no white man was supposed to have been, some Canadian popped up as a shaggy and cunning guide. Maybe only the French would have chosen to settle a landscape of marsh and rivers and lily pads. Certainly only the Scots of the Hudson's Bay Company, coming after, would have wanted to knot a lifeline across three thousand miles of tundra.

NEC·SPE·NEC·MET

2
A HOME AWAY FROM HOME

On a famous day in 1580, there was held in London a banquet in the Middle Temple, one of those "inns of court" which by Queen Elizabeth's time had become not only the law schools of England but the think-tanks and Establishment clubs, the meeting places of men who had the influence at court, and also the power and the money, to back, among other things, the English venture into the New World.

This feast was held to celebrate the return, from a two-year-and-ten-month voyage around the world, of the most unscrupulous of English pirates, a sea dog well trained by his kinsman, the slave trader Sir John Hawkins. Francis Drake was a Devon boy who went to sea in his early teens. He made daring voyages to Guinea and the Gulf of Mexico, and when he was twenty-four he received a regular privateering commission from Queen Elizabeth (whom the Pope had recently excommunicated) to sack Spanish ports and plunder Spanish treasure ships in the West Indies. He was so good at it that the Queen gave him the money to equip five small ships with a crew of one hundred and sixty-six men in order to attempt something no Englishman had ever done: enter the South Seas through the Strait of Magellan. On this astounding voyage he reached Brazil, put down a mutiny, withstood scurvy and dysentery, was tossed like a cork for fifty-two days in "a tempest . . . the like of which no traveller hath felt since Noah's flood," and ultimately found himself in the Pacific off the coast of Chile. Then he sailed north, harassing every Spanish ship he saw and ransacking the cities of Chile and Peru. He left the Pacific Coast only after going beyond San Francisco, proceeded to the Moluccas and Celebes and Java and then turned for home. He brought back so much altar plate and golden crucifixes and gleaming plunder that the *Golden Hind*, his flagship, could barely list into the home port of Plymouth. The Queen rewarded him with a knighthood. And his eminence as the best buccaneer of his age was celebrated in the Middle Temple, of which he was made an honorary member.

Drake's voyage excited the English, and not only the English court,

One of Sir Francis Drake's more notorious exploits was the seizure of the rich Spanish city of Santo Domingo in the West Indies in 1585. In this contemporary map, Drake's fleet lies in the harbor. The Spanish eventually paid a ransom and Drake sailed away.

with the vision that had finally ensnared Ferdinand and Isabella into financing Columbus: America as a land veined with gold and blazing with precious stones. The picture was filled in with much gorgeous detail by a geographer of Welsh extraction named Richard Hakluyt, who decided at an early age to devote his life to "globes, maps and spheres." Once Spain had been crippled at sea, geography became a mania with the Elizabethans, much as space movies have become since the first space flights. One of John Donne's most famous and bawdy poems—written, it should be said, before he became the Dean of Saint Paul's—describes the discovery of his mistress's body as a voyage to America ("And sailing towards her India, in that way, Shall at her fair Atlantick Navell stay"); and in another he hails his safe arrival with the triumphant line: "O My America! My New-Found-Land." Hakluyt, more of a researcher than a poet, burrowed into all the records he could find of the Spanish and French voyages and laid before the Queen a one-man encyclopedia of the wonders of America. It was, he assured everybody, a land "of huge and unknown greatness," though he himself had never been west of Bristol.

The English version of the Spanish El Dorado was more practical, and it had a wider appeal. In spite of that other myth, of Elizabeth's Merrie England, England was only just emerging as a European power. The Middle Ages were not far away: England was a land of farmers and shepherds resenting feudal taxes and tithes paid to large landowners, of mechanics and small merchants in small cities with enough slums to encourage the poor to get out of them. The Drake-Hakluyt story, as it touched the ordinary working Englishman, offered the miracle of a place to get away from it all, and it was naturally garnished with extravagant detail by every sailor in port. Ben Jonson and a couple of friends wrote a play that has a conversation between an intending emigrant, or maybe simply a goggle-eyed gossip, and a sea captain who in that year, 1605, had certainly not touched America. To the listener's doubts about whether Virginia was already inhabited by Englishmen, and whether any treasure had ever been found there, the sea captain goes off into this dithyramb:

A whole country of English is there, man . . . they have married with the Indians who are so in love with 'hem that all the treasure they have they lay at their feete . . . I tell thee, golde is more plentiful there than copper is with us . . . why, man, all their dripping pans and their chamber pottes are pure golde . . . and for rubies and diamonds, they goe forth on holydayes and gather 'hem by the seashore, to hang on their children's coates and sticke in their caps . . . And then you shall live freely there, without sargeants or courtiers or lawyers, or intelligencers.

When the time came, there was no lack of willing emigrants. It is hard to imagine a Scot, a Lancashire man, or even a native of barren Cornwall believing in chamber pots made of gold. But life was bleak for the common man, and he must have been greatly taken with these hints of a country with no recruiting sergeants and bailiffs, no spies, magistrates, tithe gatherers, or other such badgering types.

The men of substance who financed the colonies were not bemused by such fictions, but they saw the prospect of a breathtaking investment in a country that, unlike their own, had unbounded virgin land. Since all newly discovered lands belonged automatically to the Crown, the men who warmed to this enterprise had first to procure from James I a charter as a trading company. This was a joint-stock company, for individuals had learned to their cost in many lone trade ventures in Europe and the East that a private purse carried no authority abroad and was "cold comfort to adventures." So the men who jointly raised the money were such as Sir John Popham, a lord chief justice; Sir Thomas Smith, director of the East India Company; and Sir Ferdinando Gorges, governor of the fort at Plymouth. They were out to finance what they hoped would be profitable plantations in Virginia, guaranteed by the authority of the state.

Because of the commercial rivalry between the shippers of London and the provincial ports, two separate companies were organized, one for London and one for Plymouth. The backers got their charter, and while the document guaranteed such English rights as trial by jury and rights of inheritance, it left the trade and maintenance of the colonies to the backers—although, as the colony was to have the status of an overseas royal manor, it would be governed by a council approved by the Crown and its disputes would be settled by the English courts.

In 1606 three ships financed by the London Company set sail and went by the southern route past the Azores and the Canary Islands. They cruised in the West Indies and then went north, intending to settle discreetly north of the Spanish in Florida and south of the French in Canada. In April 1607 they came on Chesapeake Bay, and, after a month of inching their way past coastal Indian settlements, they entered the James River and moored in six fathoms off a wooded peninsula, which they named after the King—Jamestown. Thirty-nine of the 144 who had sailed were already dead, and the weird noises the survivors heard from the woods, as well as the sporadic appearance of Indian scouts, quickened the labor of their first job, building a stockade.

While they were at it, they must have had very rueful second thoughts about the whole adventure. They were surrounded by a malarial swamp on the edge of endless dense forest. They found very few ingredients of the cornucopia promised in a poem written by Michael Drayton on the eve of their sailing:

Virginia,
Earth's onely paradise.
Where Nature hath in store
Fowle, Venison and Fish,
And the Fruitfull'st Soyle,
Without your Toyle,
Three harvests more,
All greater than your Wish,
And the ambitious Vine,
Crownes with his purple Masse,
The cedar reaching hie
To kisse the Sky,
The Cypresse, Pine
And use-full Sassafras.

They had been taken in by the promotional literature that advertised, as always, a paradise somewhere else. They were commanded by a few sea captains and relatives of the backers, but most of them were ordinary sailors, footloose bachelors, adventurers, poor farmers, slum people, the odd gentleman, and some convicts. (If you were eager to get to America, all you had to do was steal a rabbit or swipe a cloak, do a six-month stretch, and be shipped away.)

Their growing restlessness was not pacified by the opening of the sealed orders, which prescribed the names of the president and council that would be in charge. Among the names was that of one John Smith, who was immediately expelled by a majority vote for having been mutinous on the voyage over. A parson pleaded for him, and he was grudgingly reappointed, but the incident was a small omen of big troubles to come.

In the first place (and very nearly the last), the colonists hadn't the ghost of an idea of the first rule of settlement—to be self-sustaining. They lived off the supplies they'd brought over, and they exhausted them in seven months. Then they tried to barter with the Indians or filch food and land from them. It might have seemed to the colonists that this procedure had been laid down in the London contract, but to the Indians it was theft—so now it became dangerous to forage in the interior woods, even for timber. Shiftless as ever, they actually began to chop down the houses they'd built for firewood. They bickered and stole and, lacking medicines, they died.

The first two years, in fact, were dire, and, by the time there were only thirty-eight left of the 105 who had landed, they were down to living off the animals of the woods and cadging corn from the natives. At one stage they packed up to go home and were already afloat at the mouth of the river when by a providential fluke they met an incoming ship under the

John White sailed with the first colonizing expedition to Roanoke Island in Virginia in 1585. He produced a number of drawings of Indian life like this one, which were later engraved and published. After the colony failed, White himself led a second expedition in 1587, but was forced to sail back to England for more supplies. By the time he reached Roanoke again in 1590, however, all the colonists (including his daughter and granddaughter) had vanished without trace.

Their rype corne

Their greene corne.

Corne newly sprong.

Their sitting at meate

The place of solemne Prayer.

The house wherin the Tombe of their Herounds standeth.

SECOTON.

A Ceremony in their prayers w strange testurs and songs dansing abowt posts carued on the topps lyke mens faces.

*Aboard a Spanish slaver
captured en route to the
West Indies by a British
warship, slaves huddle
among bales and barrels.
The watercolor sketch at
left was made on the spot
by a young English naval
officer. Once in America,
the more fortunate
survivors of the journey
might have ended up in
the relatively sturdy
brick-and-thatch slave
quarters of a tidewater
plantation (above).*

century, you would have noticed another novelty that took hold as the root of Southern prosperity: the heavy labor was done by blacks. We are talking about slavery.

To the Portuguese goes the melancholy privilege of having started the European enslavement of African Negroes, in 1444, fifty years before Columbus. It was systematized under the kings of Spain "to lighten the burdens" of the natives of the West Indies. The English shipped the first blacks from Africa into Virginia—on a ship bearing the ironical name of the *Jesus of Lübeck*—twelve years after the settlement. In the first forty years, however, there were no more than three hundred blacks. All the lowly labor was done by white indentured servants. But tobacco called for labor battalions, and for more drudgery than skill, and when the Virginians needed slavery they made it legal. Once the Royal African Company gave a monopoly of the slave trade to England, the blacks were shipped in legions. By the 1680s they were coming in at the rate of sixty thousand a decade.

Obviously, the market for slaves was in the South, but the men who built the ships for the traffic were in the North, and the ports of Massachusetts, Connecticut, and Rhode Island made some famous fortunes out of it. It is interesting, in a morbid way, to recall that the first moral objections came from the North, but they were soon strangled by the ship owners' profits. The first realistic objections to slavery came in the South, and there was a long and strenuous campaign to stop it. But it was not waged in the conscience of the South. It was a fear of being outnumbered, a terror of insurrection. Yet the purchase of human lives was cheap, whether of black men for the fields of America or white children for the coal mines and factories of England. And when you can buy a tame laboring population with no say in the terms of its labor, you have solved all our plaguing problems of unemployment, wages, prices, and racial minorities.

On such a base there evolved in time, in South Carolina more than anywhere, a spacious society on the English country gentleman's model, with a plantation upriver and a town house, inhabited during a social season as regular as that of London or Bath, along the waterfront of Charleston.

If the other English settlements had been run on the Southern model, if—a very big if—the Northern lands and climate had been amenable to huge, profitable single crops, there could very well have been no American Revolution, and probably no American Civil War. For the Southern colonies did not resent their control by the King's Council, and in religion they remained more or less harmoniously Church of England—even though, after thirty years or so, dissenters bristled here and there and managed to form three parishes. These dissenters became dissatisfied with the King's vicars of Christ and applied for new parsons to come down from Boston, which by then was the American capital of dissent, more accurately, of separatism. Accordingly, three ministers were sent into the conformist South. Their arrival so outraged the majority that Virginia passed a law demanding conformity to the Book of Common Prayer, and the three wise men from the Northeast hotfooted it back to Boston. It was left for Germans and Ulstermen to introduce, very much later, nonconformist churches in a tolerable form. The Southern system, however, whatever its virtues and vices, did not produce a society so radically independent of Britain that it would portend a steady drift to republicanism. That was done in another and a ruder place, by sterner men to the north.

Two years after the Jamestown landing, a ship on its way to Virginia was wrecked on an island over five hundred miles due east of Charleston, South Carolina. The island had been known to English sailors for years, but not as a desirable resort. Shakespeare talks darkly about "the vex'd Bermoothes," and to Sir Walter Raleigh the mention of Bermuda recalled "a hellish sea for thunder, lightning and stormes." But in 1612, three years after the wreck, a shipload of men, women, and sailors settled there. Their charter belonged to the London Company, which, however, had enough on its hands in Virginia, so a subsidiary group took over the running of the new colony.

The settlers were astonished to come on three men, the only survivors of the earlier wreck, who were in bouncing health, who extolled the climate and had managed very cozily in a house they had built amid a garden of vegetables and a cache of seed pearls and ambergris. The colonists fought for a while over the local supplies of ambergris, which was greatly prized as a medicine and the essence of a fine perfume. It was ambergris that saved the island economy, and by the end of 1614 there were over six hundred settlers. For some time afterwards it was much easier to raise money in London by mentioning the tonic of Bermuda than the headache of Virginia.

But having paid our respects to the second English colony, we must now come to those "ruder and sterner" men who planted the third: those immortal Pilgrims who have managed to install themselves in the popular American pantheon as not only the bravest heroes of English settlement but the first. They were a new kind of emigrant, religious dissenters who had the courage of their beliefs and the luck to come after the Jamestown disasters. The Virginia Company of London wangled a charter from the Crown and was the Pilgrims' nominal and sympathetic sponsor. Unfortunately, the Company was losing thousands in Virginia, so it could offer no extensive financial assistance. But it did make it very

A slightly fanciful nautical scene exactly contemporary with the embarkation
of the Pilgrims in 1620: "Departure of an East Indiaman," by Adam Willaerts.

Within a year Winthrop and the Puritans were ready to sail with much the largest expedition that had gone to the New World. It was meant to be subsidized by the so-called New England Company, a new grouping of backers that got a patent from the old Plymouth Company, which had been recognized as the Council of New England. But the New England Company, after settling Salem in Massachusetts, felt uncertain about the validity of its patents and decided to have them confirmed by the King. The company was reorganized by substantial Puritans who secured a royal charter for "the Company of Massachusetts Bay in New England."

Between this charter and those of all the previous settlements, there was a crucial and liberating difference. And Winthrop was responsible for it. He was not alone in fearing that, if the new settlement failed to prosper, its charter would be revoked by the King and it would become a royal province. (This had happened in Virginia.) Winthrop argued that, since anyone who bought stock in the company could vote at its meetings, the control of the colony would be at the mercy of a shifting council based in England. The accommodating clause that was inserted was deceptively trivial. It said that the stockholders were not required to meet in a particular place—that is, England—and what it meant was, in the apt summary of Charles M. Andrews, that the settlers could be sure of controlling their own affairs "by taking company and charter along with them to New England, thus swallowing up the company in the colony. In this way the company would be under Puritan control and could be manipulated to serve Puritan ends, which, Winthrop argued, were the ends of God." What it came to mean, as we shall see, is that the governor of the Company could become the governor of the colony on the spot. Winthrop was chosen as the one and elected as the other.

He sailed, in March 1630, in the flagship of a fleet of four ships, carrying over five hundred men, women, and children, whom Winthrop tenderly thought of as a noble microcosm of the human family—*his* family, for he carried the company charter in his pocket. In Massachusetts he planted the first truly self-governing colony. If any one man can be called the Founding Father of New England, he is it.

While the Puritans were concerned in planting "a city of God," they also had to eat. Winthrop was the last man to see any conflict between prosperity and prayer. He epitomizes several bred-in-the-bone convictions that we don't today associate with Puritanism. He believed, for instance, that hunting with a gun was wrong only if you couldn't make a profit from the kill. He thought it would be wrong to move to New England unless the colony could guarantee a financial success. It was a man's duty to God to use his talents to the full. His material success would be the visible sign of God's blessing.

So, once arrived, the children of God raised cattle, and Indian corn and

John Winthrop, the first governor of the Massachusetts Bay Colony, cultivated an air of Puritan authority and rectitude for this portrait, which was painted in the 1640s.

vegetables for their own sustenance; but they looked to more profitable work later on and kept a long credit line out to the London merchants. They soon got busy in the fur trade, and at Marblehead they set up an industry that was as much their salvation as tobacco had been the Virginians'—"the sacred cod." (It soon replaced the royal coat of arms as an official Massachusetts emblem, and today it dominates the hallway of the lower house of the government of the state, the body that holds the purse strings.)

Winthrop had an almost inquisitorial concern for the saintliness of the rulers of the colony, but he was never fussy about the purity of the customer. His steady belief that virtue paid dividends made him rejoice whenever Yankee ships went off to deliver a cargo of codfish—even when the buyers were Roman Catholics, because they paid better than anybody. And when the English Civil War halted emigration, the Puritans—finding their work force frozen—apparently felt no qualms about going into the more profitable business still of building ships and loading them with fish and beef and vegetables for the sustenance of the slave-holding planters who grew a single crop of tobacco or sugar in the West Indies. (It was only the first of many noble American life styles supported by dubious means.)

Massachusetts, then, began to flourish by the business acumen of its founders. But it achieved stability, and ultimately independence, through a form of government that was severe but on the whole just. It was unquestionably more representative than anything the Puritans had known in England. Winthrop told an early meeting of the settlers why, by his lights, Virginia had failed: "Its main end was carnal, not religious. It gathered a multitude of rude persons and it failed to set up a right form of government." Like most Puritans before and since, Winthrop knew what was right for other people, and he was there to see that they got it. Yet to his great credit he set up a government growing out of the company charter that was later susceptible even to the pressures of democracy, a form of government that, in Winthrop's decided opinion, "amongst civil nations is accounted the meanest and worst." Samuel Eliot Morison has acutely remarked that the Massachusetts government fashioned the mold of "the standard American pattern" and was very similar to that of the typical American business corporation:

As a business charter, the corporation consisted of freemen (stockholders), meeting in an assembly called the General Court where were annually elected, on a stated date, the governor, deputy governor, and assistants (councillors). But transfer overseas turned the company into a colonial government. The freemen were now the voters, the governor and deputy governor the two chief magistrates, and the assistants doubled as governor's council and supreme court. By 1644, owing to a typical small-town dispute over a stray sow, the

A rare survivor of the days when the wilderness began a few miles west of the New England coast, the Parson Capen house still stands on its hillock in Topsfield, Massachusetts. Built in 1684, its diamond-paned windows, steep gabled roof, and overhanging upper story are characteristic of the simple Jacobean architecture brought into the New World by the first settlers.

In the mid-eighteenth century, Boston's squares and public buildings looked exactly like those of London. The Old State House (center) was supplanted soon after the Revolution by Charles Bulfinch's grand gold-domed structure now standing atop Beacon Hill.

threats of parliamentary control, after England got a Parliament again in the 1660s. (The independence of the colony had been greatly helped by the lack of a strong central government in England before and during the Civil War.) He gave every waking moment, usually from an hour before dawn to midnight, to the guidance of the colony. The best proof of his skill and benevolence is the fact that he was twelve times elected as governor of the colony and died, in 1649 at the age of sixty-one, in office.

Between the two strong and opposing cultures of Virginia and New England, the only continuous highway was the sea. By land there lay five hundred miles of roads so primitive that the leading men of Richmond and Boston knew London better than they knew each other. Charleston, South Carolina, was as far from Boston as Vienna is from Plymouth; and those two cities are hardly more dissimilar than the societies created in the South and the North. The early model of New England could hardly have worked in the rest of the country, and neither could the early model of Virginia.

But the English, though often seized with odd delusions, are never obsessed for long with a single formula for salvation or society. They have tended to distrust magic remedies and hypnotic leaders and preferred moderate solutions that allow a lot of different types to be their dotty selves. So there came into being a string of Middle Colonies—New York, Pennsylvania, Maryland, Delaware—whose only original links were the English language, the English common law, and an itch to start afresh, for various reasons, in the New World. Like all middlemen—like Sweden always lying between two monolithic powers—they tended to neutrality and tolerance. Or, to put it the other way round, tolerant men tended to congregate in the hinterland that lay comfortably remote from the rigors of Puritan conformity and the uniformity of the Anglican, plantation South. Pennsylvania was founded because Charles II owed £16,000 to a dead admiral who, alive, had been grieved by his son's embrace of the Quakers and by his frequent wrangles with the Establishment. The King was happy to get rid of this son, William Penn, by settling the debt with a grant of land in America, very fertile and bursting with minerals, no less than three hundred miles long and one hundred and sixty miles wide! Maryland was set up because one of the King's ambassadors turned Catholic and wanted to make things safe for Catholics in America.

So through the late seventeenth and early eighteenth centuries, the various English spread themselves in the Middle Colonies and welcomed

As shown in this engraving, dated 1752, Baltimore was little more than a small coastal settlement where men could net fish in the shallows along the shore.

German Lutherans and Swedish Protestants, Moravians and Jacobites, Mennonites and Jews. By 1733 there were thirteen colonies settled along the Atlantic seaboard—in order of founding Virginia, Massachusetts, New Hampshire, New York, Connecticut, Maryland, Rhode Island, Delaware, Pennsylvania, North Carolina, New Jersey, South Carolina, and Georgia. Each had its own government, its own currency, its own trade laws and religious ways. They were, indeed, long before the Revolution, more like thirteen nations, enjoying or suffering every sort of relationship with the interior Indians from undisturbed friendship to murderous hostility.

It was the Middle Colonies that produced the most flexible societies, curiously classless and homogeneous, in which at the end of the day the parson and the tallow chandler, the baker, the bricklayer, and the banker seemed to reach instinctively for the same diversions: a little fiddle playing, a game of cards, the chanting of a ballad about the capture of the latest pirate, talk about politics and women and predestination, or a respectful reading of an admired sermon. Pennsylvania bred independent large farmers without slaves, and, although its establishment was Quaker, a dozen religious sects lived there without conflict or bigotry. In particular, the middle city of Philadelphia was probably the most civilized, by any modern definition, of colonial capitals. Here had developed a human type odd enough to make an English visitor write, in the middle of the eighteenth century, about a kind of scholar-citizen, politically alert, "whose learning is, however, always ingenious and useful."

Thus, three main cultures emerged from the English settlements. The planter society of the South, with a fluid aristocracy very open to labor and talent. The more egalitarian settlements of New England, controlled, however, by a Puritan oligarchy. And the greatly varied Middle Colonies, reaching from New York to the Virginia border, which were at once agrarian and mercantile and gave birth to the first cities, the first businessmen, a string of ports, and a range of trades from printer-publishers to skilled workmen.

These divisions were very clear to the people who lived within them, and provided the visiting English with a rough breakdown of the colonial system that could keep them from making elementary blunders in dealing with any one of the three types of society. But just as, today, Englishmen are always deaf to the social implications of the American accents they mingle with (even Peter Ustinov's mimic Americans—whether admirals, New England bluebloods, businessmen, or Hollywood agents—are always Midwesterners and usually sound like gangsters), so the English of the middle eighteenth century were, on the whole, deaf and blind to the subtle but strong and growing characteristics that were making Americans of these transplanted Englishmen. There were precious few Englishmen in Parliament or elsewhere who sensed the powerful drift of such strange American novelties as the town meeting, the abolition of primogeniture, the custom of electing rather than appointing officers in the state militias. Fewer still pondered the strangeness of some fundamental things noted by an admiring French immigrant: landowners without tenants, and farmers who had never heard of a peasant. If more Englishmen had sensed the possibility of a break with Europe that these characteristics portended, they might have echoed with a more ominous inflection Crèvecoeur's immortal question: "What, then, is the American, this new man?"

3
MAKING A
REVOLUTION

It is fair to say that the vast majority of Americans have no doubts about the rightness of the colonists' break with England. The phrase "the American Revolution" causes a certain glow even in the most entrenched conservatives, who would never revolt against anybody except a new revolutionary and who, in the Revolutionary War, would most probably have been on the Loyalist side. This is because Americans are taught a very simple view of their revolution—that it was a straightforward crusade against a tyrannical Parliament and a hysterical king an ocean away. Of course, no revolution was ever so simple, certainly not this one. But patriotism, a bad historian, writes the most beguiling history, since it always offers a flattering explanation of a complicated story and satisfies our insatiable hunger for good guys and bad guys.

In the middle eighteenth century, the nation that was to rebel was hardly a nation at all but a string of separate, and separately governed, colonies reaching down the Atlantic seaboard fourteen hundred miles or so from northern Massachusetts (what is now Maine) through Georgia—in one place a royal colony, in another a barony, in a third a land-grant company. The laws of each were administered by a royal governor, or by planters, or by shippers, or by clergymen, or by Quaker "peacemakers." Their ways of work were dictated by different economies, by fisheries or by farming, by rice and indigo or by tobacco, or by turning molasses into rum and bartering it for English goods. Most of the colonials, if they had visited each other much, would have felt themselves to be in a foreign land. Like most nations living on the same continent, they quarreled a good deal. Who owned this river? Who had the right to the oyster catch in this bay? Where did the border lie between Pennsylvania and Maryland? (That caused such a rumpus that two of the King's surveyors came over to settle what threatened to turn into a border war. Their names were Charles Mason and Jeremiah Dixon.)

It has often been said that for a century and a half the strongest link between the colonies was their common allegiance to the King of England, which we certainly should not "belittle" (to use an Americanism of Jefferson's much ridiculed at the time in England). The colonists may not have made much of this allegiance, but, until the figure of George III was inflated by caricature into a tyrant, most of them would not have doubted that allegiance either. The stronger link was their inheritance of the English common law. But the strongest of all was the slowly growing knowledge that they had all shared the strange experience of living on a new continent and that, in the generations since 1607, they had changed from Englishmen, possessing interesting variations on the originals, into Americans.

The pull away from English institutions, and especially English law, took longer than the slow but more irrevocable departure from English folkways. But in the weaning of colonies and empires from the mother country there is usually a moment of organic change, an "episode" as the doctors call it, which is seen only later to have been decisive. Such an episode was the final attempt of the French, between 1754 and 1760, to confine the English colonies to the lands east of the Appalachians, and to hold the hinterland and prepare it for an American empire of their own.

For, while the English colonies were settling and prospering, the French were by no means abandoning their aim of establishing an interior empire based upon the Mississippi Valley. They were holding the Great Lakes and fighting the reinvigorated Iroquois and the Seneca; and in the South they were trading with the Indians and hoping one day to join the two ends of their settlements and outposts. They could do this only by securing control of the valley of the Ohio, the essential link between Canada and the Mississippi. For many decades they were busy quickening the trade of the lakes and rivers, and incidentally developing military mobility by building hundreds of bateaux larger and swifter than anything the English colonists knew. Forty feet long, nine feet wide, they could carry forty or fifty men, cannon, and provisions for a month or more.

Whenever England and France were threatening each other with war in Europe, or were actually at it, the French in Canada made sporadic and lethal raids on the frontier settlements of the New England colonies. And from time to time the New Englanders retaliated with northern expeditions (John Winthrop's grandson led one against Montreal). They always failed.

At the end of the 1740s, the French decided to stake out their main claim, literally. An expedition rolled down the Ohio River and buried lead plates at intervals to mark their territorial possession. At that moment, an English company of Virginia planters with a royal patent was surveying the same territory. The time had come, the French realized, to stop such English incursions. From the present site of Erie, Pennsylvania, down through western Pennsylvania and the Ohio all the way to the mouth of the Mississippi, therefore, they built a chain of impressive forts.

The vital link between the Mississippi and the Ohio Valley was the spot where the Monongahela and the Allegheny rivers met. The English already had a rude fort there, but in 1754 the French destroyed it and built Fort Duquesne. It was from this base that the French marched to their first open clash with the Virginians, who sent out a small force under the command of a newly commissioned, twenty-one-year-old lieutenant-colonel. He scarcely had time to build a primitive fort in a river bottom before the French overwhelmed him.

Luckily, the French were gallant enough to let the surviving Virginians go home disarmed. Their twenty-one-year-old commander, a country squire named George Washington, was humiliated but not cast down. As refreshed by the smell of battle as the young Churchill in a later river war, he wrote afterwards: "I have heard the bullets whistle and, believe me, there is something charming in the sound." It was to charm him for the next six years.

The following year the war was really on when Edward Braddock, a Scottish major-general in the Coldstream Guards, hacked his way with a much larger British and colonial force several hundred miles through the mountain wilderness to take Fort Duquesne. The French and their Indian allies ambushed and killed him, and routed his army. This disaster roused London to the realization that it had a full-scale war on its hands. A large expeditionary force commanded by a flock of English generals was sent over to pierce the French lines along the enormous reach of the rivers. But there were fewer lines than redoubts, at strategic clearings in a wilderness. It was not a kind of warfare to which the English had been accustomed, though it taught them something about the strange horrors they were to encounter in the Revolutionary War. They suffered atrociously in the mountains and the forests from the Indian guerrillas, and in the pitched battles they were up against superior generalship. At Fort Ticonderoga in upstate New York, three thousand Frenchmen under Montcalm stood off fifteen thousand British and colonial troops, and the Black Watch suffered the worst losses in the history of the regiment until the Second Battle of the Somme.

It took six years before Quebec and Montreal surrendered to the British and the fighting virtually ended in North America. Three years later, in 1763, Canada and her dependencies and the whole interior "empire" of France were transferred to the Crown of England. Florida

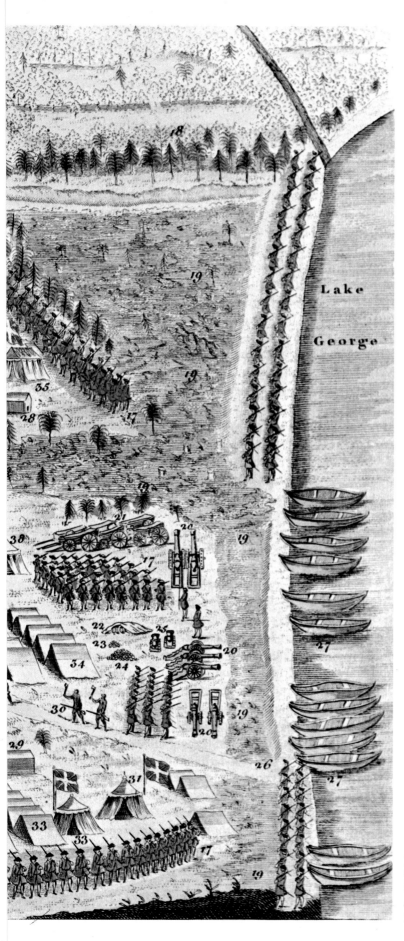

Lake

George

In 1755, on Lake George in upstate
New York, French troops and their Indian
allies attacked a British encampment.
They were driven off with heavy losses.

an Account of a late Military Massacre at Boston, or the Consequences of Quartering Troops in a populous well-regulated Town, taken from t

The BLOODY MASSACRE perpetrated in King-Street BOSTON on March 5th 1770 by a party of the 29th REG

Unhappy BOSTON! see thy Sons deplore,
Thy hallow'd Walks besmear'd with guiltless Gore:
While faithless P—n and his savage Bands,
With murd'rous Rancour stretch their bloody Hands;
Like fierce Barbarians grinning o'er their Prey,
Approve the Carnage, and enjoy the Day.

If scalding drops from Rage from Anguish Wrung
If speechless Sorrows lab'ring for a Tongue,
Or if a weeping World can ought appease
The plaintive Ghosts of Victims such as these;
The Patriot's copious Tears for each are shed,
A glorious Tribute which embalms the Dead.

But know, FATE summons to that awful G
Where JUSTICE strips the Murd'rer of his
Should venal C—ts the scandal of the L
Snatch the relentless Villain from her H
Keen Execrations on this Plate inscr
Shall reach a JUDGE who never can be

The unhappy Sufferers were Mess.rs SAM.L GRAY, SAM.L MAVERICK, JAM.S CALDWELL, CRISPUS ATTUCKS & PAT.
Killed. Six wounded; two of them (CHRIST.R MONK & JOHN CLARK) *Mortally*

BOSTON, March 12, 1770.

THE Town of Boston affords a recent and melancholy Demonstration of the destructive Consequences of quartering Troops among Citizens in a Time of Peace, under a Pretence of supporting the Laws and aiding Civil Authority; every considerate and unprejudic'd Person among us was deeply imprest with the Apprehension of these Consequences when it was known that a Number of Regiments were ordered to this Town under such a Pretext, but in Reality to inforce oppressive Measures; to awe and controul the legislative as well as executive Power of the Province, and to quell a Spirit of Liberty, which however it may have been basely oppos'd and even ridicul'd by some, would do Honor to any Age or Country. A few Persons amongst us had determin'd to use all their Influence to procure so destructive a Measure with a View to their securely enjoying the Profits of an American Revenue, and unhappily both for Britain and this Country they found Means to effect it.

It is to Governor Bernard, the Commissioners, their Confidents and Coadjutors, that we are indebted as the procuring Cause of a military Power in this Capital—The Boston Journal of Occurrences, as printed in Mr. Holt's York Gazette, from Time to Time, afforded many striking Instances of the Distresses brought upon the Inhabitants by this Measure; and since those Journals have been discontinued, our Troubles from that Quarter have been growing upon us: We have known a Party of Soldiers in the face of Day fire off a loaden Musket upon the Inhabitants, others have been prick'd with their Bayonets, and even our Magistrates assaulted and put in Danger of their Lives, when Offenders brought before them have been rescued; and why those and other bold and base Criminals have as yet escaped the Punishment due to their Crimes, may be soon Matter of Enquiry by the Representative Body of this People—It is natural to suppose that when the Inhabitants of this Town saw those Laws which had been enacted for their Security, and which they were ambitious of holding up to the Soldiery, eluded, they should more commonly resent for themselves—and accordingly it has so happened; many have been the Squabbles between them and the Soldiery; but it seems their being often worsted by our Youth in those Rencounters, has only serv'd to irritate the former—What passed at Mr. Gray's Rope-walk, has already been given the Public, and may be said to have led the Way to the late Catastrophe—That the Rope-walk Lads when attaked by superior Numbers should defend themselves with so much Spirit and Success in the Club-way, was too mortifying, and perhaps it may hereafter appear, that even some of their Officers were *unhappily* affected with this Circumstance: Divers Stories were propagated among the Soldiery, that serv'd to agitate their Spirits; particularly on the Sabbath, that one Chambers, a Serjeant, represented as a sober Man, had been missing the preceeding Day, and must therefore have been murdered by the Townsmen; an Officer of Distinction so far credited this Report, that he enter'd Mr. Gray's Rope-walk that Sabbath; and when required of by that Gentleman as soon as he could meet him, the Occasion of his so doing, the Officer reply'd, that it was to look if the Sergeant said to be murdered had not been hid there; this sober Sergeant was found on the Monday unhurt, in a House of Pleasure—The Evidences already collected shew, that many Threatnings had been thrown out by the Soldiery, but we do not pretend to say that there was any preconcerted Plan, when the Evidences are published, the World will judge—We may however venture to declare, that it appears too probable from their Conduct, that some of the Soldiery aimed to draw and provoke the Townsmen into Squabbles, and that they then intended to make Use of other Weapons than Canes, Clubs or Bludgeons.

Our Readers will doubtless expect a circumstantial Account of the tragical Affair on Monday Night last; but we hope they will excuse our being so particular as we should have been, had we not seen that the Town was intending an Enquiry and full Representation thereof.

On the Evening of Monday, being the 5th Current, several Soldiers of the 29th Regiment were seen parading the Streets with their drawn Cutlasses and Bayonets, abusing and wounding Numbers of the Inhabitants.

A few minutes after nine o'clock, four youths, named Edward Archbald, William Merchant, Francis Archbald, and John Leech, jun. came down Cornhill together, and seperating at Doctor Loring's corner, the two former were passing the narrow alley leading to Murray's barrack, in which was a soldier brandishing a broad sword of an uncommon size against the walls out of which he struck fire plentifully. A person of a mean countenance armed with a large cudgel bore him company. Edward Archbald admonished Mr. Merchant to take care of the sword, on which the soldier turned round and struck Archbald on the arm, then pushed at Merchant and pierced thro' his cloaths inside the arm close to the arm-pit and grazed the skin. Merchant then struck the soldier with a short stick he had, and the other Person ran to the barrack and bro't with him two soldiers, one armed with a pair of tongs the other with a shovel: he with the tongs pursued Archbald back thro' the alley, collar'd and laid him over the head with the tongs. The noise bro't people together, and John Hicks, a young lad, coming up, knock'd the soldier down, but let him get up again; and more lads gathering, drove them back to the barrack, where the boys stood some time as it were to keep them in. In less than a minute 10 or 12 of them came out with drawn cutlasses, clubs & bayonets, and set upon the unarmed boys and young folks, who stood them a little while, but finding the inequality of their equipment dispersed.—On hearing the noise, one Samuel Atwood, came up to see what was the matter, and entering the alley from dock-square, heard the latter part of the combat, and when the boys had dispersed he met the 10 or 12 soldiers aforesaid rushing down the alley towards the square, and asked them if they intended to murder people? They answered Yes, by G—d, root and branch! With that one of them struck Mr. Atwood with a club, which was repeated by another, and being unarmed he turned to go off, and received a wound on the left shoulder which reached the bone and gave him much pain. Retreating a few steps, Mr. Atwood met two officers and said, Gentlemen, what is the matter? They answered, you'll see by and by. Immediately after, those heroes appeared in the square, asking where were the boogers? where were the cowards? But notwithstanding their fierceness to naked men, one of them advanced towards a youth who had a split of a raw stave in his hand, and said damn them here is one of them; but the young man seeing a person near him with a drawn sword and good cane ready to support him, held up his stave in defiance, and they quietly passed by him up the little alley by Mr. Silsby's to Kingstreet, where they attacked single and unarmed persons till they raised much clamor, and then turned down Cornhill street, insulting all they met in like manner, and pursuing some to their very doors. Thirty or forty persons mostly lads, being by this means gathered in King street, Capt. Preston, with a party of men with charged bayonets, came from the main guard to the commissioners house, the soldiers pushing their bayonets, crying, Make way! They took place by the custom-house, and continuing to push to drive the people off, pricked some in several places; on which they were clamorous, and, it is said, threw snow-balls. On this, the Captain commanded them to fire, and more snow-balls coming, he again said, Damn you, Fire, be the consequence what it will! One soldier then fired, and a townsman with a cudgel struck him over the hands with such force that he dropt his firelock; and rushing forward aimed a blow at the Captain's head, which graz'd his hat and fell pretty heavy upon his arm: However, the soldiers continued the fire, successively, till 7 or 8, or as some say 11 guns were discharged.

By this fatal manœuvre, three men were laid dead on the spot, and two more struggling for life; but what shewed a degree of cruelty unknown to British troops, at least since the house of Hanover has directed their operations, was an attempt to fire upon or push with their bayonets the persons who undertook to remove the slain and wounded!

Mr. Benjamin Leigh, now undertaker in the Delph Manufactory, came up, and after some conversation with Capt. Preston, relative to his conduct in this affair, advised him to draw off his men, with which he complied.

The dead are Mr. Samuel Gray, killed on the spot, the ball entering his head and beating off a large portion of his skull.

A mulatto man, named Crispus Attucks, who was born in Framingham, but lately belonged to New-Providence and was here in order to go for North-Carolina, also killed instantly; two balls entering his breast, one of them in special goring the right lobe of the lungs, and a great part of the liver most horribly.

Mr. James Caldwell, mate of Capt. Morton's vessel, in like manner killed by two balls entering his back.

Mr. Samuel Maverick, a promising youth of 17 years of age, son of the Widow Maverick, and an apprentice to Mr. Greenwood, Ivory-Turner, mortally wounded, a ball went through his belly, and was cut out at his back: He died the next morning.

A lad named Christopher Monk, about 17 years of age, an apprentice to Mr. Walker, Shipwright; wounded a ball entered his back about 4 inches above the left kidney, near the spine, and was cut out of the breast on the same side; apprehended he will die.

A lad named John Clark, about 17 years of age, whose parents live at Medford, and an apprentice to Capt. Samuel Howard of this town; wounded, a ball entered just above his groin and came out at his hip, on the opposite side, apprehended he will die.

Mr. Edward Payne, of this town, Merchant, standing at his entry-door, received a ball in his arm, shattered some of the bones.

Mr. John Green, Taylor, coming up Leverett's Lane, received a ball just under his hip, and lodged in the under part of his thigh, which was extracted.

Mr. Robert Patterson, a seafaring man, who was the person that had his trowsers shot through in Richardson's affair, wounded; a ball went thro' his right arm, and he suffered great loss of blood.

Mr. Patrick Carr, about 30 years of age, who work'd with Mr. Field Leather-Breeches-maker in Queen-street, wounded, a ball enter'd near his hip and went out at his side.

A lad named David Parker, an apprentice to Mr. Eddy the Wheelwright, wounded, a ball entered in his thigh.

The People were immediately alarmed with the Report of this horrid Massacre, the Bells were set a Ringing, and great Numbers soon assembled at the Place where this tragical Scene had been acted; their Feelings may be better conceived than express'd; and while some were taking Care of the Dead and Wounded, the Rest were in Consultation what to do in those dreadful Circumstances.—But so little intimidated where they, notwithstanding their being within a few Yards of the Main-Guard, and seeing the 29th Regiment under Arms, and drawn up in King-Street; that they kept their Station and appear'd as an Officer of Rank express'd it, ready to run upon the very Muzzles of their Muskets.—The Lieut. Governor soon came into the Town-House, and there met some of his Majesty's Council, and a Number of Civil Magistrates; a considerable Body of the People immediately entered the Council Chamber, and expressed themselves to his Honor with a Freedom and Warmth becoming the occasion. He used his utmost Endeavours to pacify them, requesting that they would let the Matter subside for the Night, and promising to do all in his Power that Justice should be done, and the Law have its Course; Men of Influence and Weight with the People were not wanting on their part to procure their Compliance with his Honor's Request by repres[enting] the horrible Consequences of a promisc[uous] rash Engagement in the Night, and assur[ing] that such Measures should be entered upon [in the] Morning as would be agreeable to their D[ignity] and a more likely way of obtaining the b[est sa]tisfaction for the Blood of their Fellow-Tow[nsmen] —The Inhabitants attended to these Sugg[estions] and the Regiment under Arms being orde[red to] their Barracks, which was insisted upon by th[e Peo]ple, they then separated and returned to their [Dwel]lings by One o'Clock, at 3 o'Clock Capt. P[reston] was committed, as were the Soldiers who f[ired a] few Hours after him.

Tuesday Morning presented a most sho[cking] Scene, the Blood of our Fellow Citizens ru[nning] like Water thro' King-Street, and the Merc[hants] Exchange the principal Spot of the Milita[ry Pa]rade for about 18 Months past. Our Blood [might] also be track'd up to the Head of Long-Lan[e, and] through divers other Streets and Passages.

At eleven o'clock the inhabitants met at F[aneu]il-Hall, and after some animated Speeches b[ecom]ing the occasion, they chose a Committee [of] respectable Gentlemen to wait upon the Lieu[t. Go]vernor in Council, to request of him to issue h[is or]ders for the immediate removal of the troo[ps.]

The Message was in these Words:

THAT it is the unanimous opinion of this [meet]ing that the inhabitants and soldiery [can no] longer live together in safety; that nothing c[an ra]tionally be expected to restore the peace of [the town] and prevent further blood and carnage, but [the im]mediate removal of the Troops; and that we [there]fore most fervently pray his Honor that his [power] and influence may be exerted for their instant [remo]val.

His Honor's Reply, which was laid befo[re the] Town then Adjourn'd to the Old South [Meet]ing-House, was as follows,

Gentlemen,

I AM extremely sorry for the unhappy aff[air] between the inhabitants and troops, and esp[ecially] for the action of the last evening, and I have [exert]ed myself upon that occasion that a due enqui[ry may] be made, and that the law may have its cou[rse. I] have in council consulted with the command[ing offi]cers of the two regiments who are in the [town.] They have their orders from the General at [New] York. It is not in my power to countermand [those] orders. The Council have desired that the t[wo re]giments may be removed to the Castle. Fr[om the] particular concern which the 29th regiment [has had] in your differences, Col. Dalrymple who is th[e com]manding officer of the troops has signified that t[hat re]giment shall without delay be placed in the b[arracks] at the Castle until he can send to the Gener[al and] receive his further orders concerning both th[e regi]ments, and that the main guard shall be re[moved,] and the 14th regiment so disposed and laid und[er such] restraint that all occasion of future disturban[ces may] be prevented.

Gazette, of March 12, 1770.

he foregoing Reply having been read and considered—the question was put, Whether the same be satisfactory? Passed in the Negative, (nem. dissentient) out of upwards of upwards Voters.

was then moved & voted that John Hancock, Mr. Samuel Adams, Mr. William Molineux, ..., Dr. Joseph Warren, Jo-Henshaw, Esq; and Samuel Pemberton, Esq; Committee to wait on his Honour the Lieut. ernor, and inform him, that it is the unani-s Opinion of this Meeting, that the Reply made Vote of the Inhabitants presented his Honor Morning, is by no means satisfactory; and nothing less will satisfy, than a total and immediate removal of all the Troops.

he Committee having waited upon the Lieut. ernor agreeable to the foregoing Vote; laid be the Inhabitants the following Vote of Council ived from his Honor.

In Honor the Lieut. Governor laid before the d a Vote of the Town of Boston, passed this noon, and then addressed the Board as follows. *Gentlemen of the Council,*

I lay before you a Vote of the Town of Bos-which I have just now received from them, I now ask your Advice what you judge proper to be done upon it.

he Council thereupon expressed themselves to animously, of opinion, "that it was absolutely sary for his Majesty's service, the good order e Town, and the peace of the Province, that Troops should be immediately removed out of Town of Boston, and thereupon advised his r to communicate this Advice of the Council l. Dalrymple, and to pray that he would or-he Troops down to Castle William." The mittee also informed the Town, that Col. Dal-le, after having seen the Vote of Council, said e Committee, "That he now gave his word onor that he would begin his Preparations in Morning, and that there should be no unne-y delay until the whole of the two Regiments removed to the Castle."

pon the above Report being read, the Inhabi-could not avoid expressing the high Satisfac-it afforded them.

er Measures were taken for the Security of Town in the Night by a strong Military ch, the Meeting was Dissolved.

he 29th Regiment have already left us, and th Regiment are following them, so that we the Town will soon be clear of all the ps. The Wisdom and true Policy of his ty's Council and Col. Dalrymple the Com-der appear in this Measure. Two Regiments e midst of this populous City; and the Inha-ts justly incensed: Those of the neighbour-Towns actually under Arms upon the first Re of the Massacre, and the Signal only wanting ing in a few Hours to the Gates of this City Thousands of our brave Brethren in the try, deeply affected with our Distresses, and hom we are greatly obliged on this Occasion o one knows where this would have ended, and important Consequences even to the whole Empire might have followed, which our ration and Loyalty upon so trying an Occa-and our Faith in the Commander's Assurance happily prevented.

st Thursday, agreeable to a general Request Inhabitants, and by the Consent of Parents Friends, were carried to their Grave in Suc-n, the Bodies of *Samuel Gray, Samuel Ma-k, James Caldwell,* and *Crispus Attucks,* the ppy Victims who fell in the bloody Massacre Monday Evening preceeding!

n this Occasion most of the Shops in Town were all the Bells were ordered to toll a solemn as were also those in the neighboring Towns arlestown, Roxbury, &c. The Procession be-to move between the Hours of 4 and 5 in the noon; two of the unfortunate Sufferers, viz. James Caldwell and Crispus Attucks, who Strangers, borne from Faneuil-Hall, attend-a numerous Train of Persons of all Ranks; the other two, viz. Mr. Samuel Gray, from louse of Benjamin Gray, (his Brother) on the h-side the Exchange, and Mr. Maverick, from louse of his distressed Mother Mrs. Mary Ma-t, in Union-Street, each followed by their res-e Relations and Friends: The several Hear-rming a Junction in King-Street, the Theatre inhuman Tragedy, proceeded from thence the Main-Street, lengthened by an immense ourse of People, so closely as to be obliged llow in Ranks of six, and brought up by a Train of Carriages belonging to the principal ry of the Town. The bodies were deposited e Vault in the middle Burying-ground: The avated Circumstances of their Death, the Dis-and Sorrow visible in every Countenance, to-r with the peculiar Solemnity with which the Funeral was conducted, surpass Description.

BOSTON, March 19.

Last Wednesday Night died, Pa-trick Carr, an Inhabitant of this Town, of the Wound he received in King-Street on the bloody and execrable Night of the 5th Instant—He had just before left his Home, and upon his coming into the Street received the fatal Ball in his Hip which passed out at the opposite Side; this is the fifth Life that has been sacrificed by the Rage of the Soldiery, but it is teared it will not be the last, as several re dangerously languishing of their Wounds. xar ains were attended on Saturday last from il-Hall by a numerous and respectable Train ourners, to the same Grave, in which those ell by the same Hands of Violence were in-the last Week.

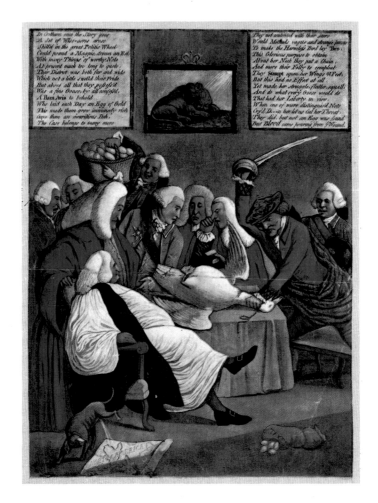

The broadside was a favorite form of political propaganda on both sides of the Atlantic before and during the American Revolution. At left, a vigorously stated account of the Boston Massacre; above, a cartoon sold in London showing that not all British opinion favored the government policy of stern measures against the colonies.

sunk in the wall of a cemetery. It says: "In defense of American independence at the Battle of Ridgefield, April 27th, 1777, died Eight Patriots who were laid in this ground, Companioned by Sixteen British Soldiers, Living, their enemies, Dying, their guests."

The British arrived as a professional army expecting, with companies of German mercenaries, to fight European set battles. Not enough of them had learned, at first or second hand, the lessons of the French and Indian Wars. The Americans were at once too shrewd and too untrained to oblige them with an Old World war. First of all, as John Adams said, the colonial population divided up into one third that took to arms, one third that was either openly or secretly loyal to the British, and one third that didn't give a damn—not the best recipe for a disciplined national army. So against the army of British regulars there stood—besides some French volunteers, immensely valuable as professionals at the start—mainly a large, improvised force of farmers, mechanics, tradesmen, parsons, lawyers, grocers, hunters, trappers, con men, thieves, and hoodlums. "Never," their sorrowing commander was to lament when the going was bad, "such a rabble dignified by the name of army." How could they even hold off for six years, much less defeat, one of the crack armies of Europe?

For one thing, there was weaponry. The British for the most part used smooth-bore muskets that allowed a lateral error of three feet at a hundred yards range. The British infantryman was not trained to pick off single targets; he stood shoulder to shoulder with his fellows and they sprayed, shall we say, in the general direction of the enemy! The Americans had smooth-bore muskets, too, but as the war moved into the interior the British came up against the frontiersmen, who did not use guns for sport. Their very existence depended on shooting their food on the wing and saving their families by picking off Indians in night raids. They needed a weapon that was light and accurate and found it in the Pennsylvania flintlock, developed for them by German settlers in Pennsylvania who doubled the length of the barrel and grooved it to make the bullet spin and stay on line. (From this rifling of the barrel comes the word "rifle.") It could not, however, be fixed with a bayonet.

But at long range, this weapon did bloody damage to shoulder-to-shoulder infantry. A Pennsylvania Tory who had seen it at work wrote a letter to a London newspaper offering rather chill advice: "This province has raised a thousand riflemen, the worst of whom will put a rifle ball into a man's head at a hundred and fifty or two hundred yards. Therefore, advise your officers who shall hereafter come out to America to settle their affairs in England before their departure." This reputation for sharpshooting was magnified in England into a witch's curse, and there were some lively desertions among men drafted for service in the

109

Colonies. It is, on the whole, an all-too-true American myth: that legendary reputation for spotting the bull's eye which began with the embattled farmers and was sustained down the next century and a half by Wyatt Earp, Wild Bill Hickok, Annie Oakley, and Sergeant York. It is a romantic tradition that dies hard, and there is a lucrative industry in suggesting to sportsmen and country boys—and, unfortunately, to malcontents and psychotics also—that whether or not you are a fast man with a buck, you too can be a fast man on the draw.

A British commander sent home a short report that was read in the House of Commons. The gist of it was: "The Americans will not stand and fight." They were jack-in-the-box guerrillas who would fight like devils for a day and a night and then go home and harvest their crops on the weekend. They would return, not always in any discernible formation, and after a swift onslaught vanish into the country by night, and then again at some unpredictable time come whizzing in like hornets. What baffled and eventually broke the British was what broke the Roman armies in their late campaigns against the barbarians, and for so long frustrated the American army in Vietnam. Edward Gibbon said it in a single passage: "All things became adverse to the Romans . . . their armour heavy, the waters deep; nor could they wield, in that uneasy situation, their weighty javelins. The barbarians, on the contrary, were enured to encounters in the bogs." Or as William Pitt sadly commented, looking at his drawn battle-lines on an alien wilderness: "You cannot conquer a map."

There is a further, and less dramatic, explanation for the colonists' survival and victory. It was the consequence of one of the most perceptive deals in American history. When the war began it was fought for a time mainly in Massachusetts and the bordering North. It didn't take the men of Massachusetts long to know it and resent it. If it was to be a continental war, the South too would have to be visibly engaged. Virginia was rich and Massachusetts was chronically short of the money for arms and supplies (like the other colonies, it never managed to pay the soldiers for long). John Adams had the notion that if a continental commander could be appointed, and he was a Virginian, then the North and the South and the Middle Colonies would have a palpable, breathing symbol of a common cause. A good deal would depend, of course, on the chosen man. Adams used his great influence with the wartime Congress now formed, first to push the idea of a continental command and then to see that it went to the man of his choice.

He was that same officer who had heard "the bullets whistle" in the first brush of the French and Indian Wars: George Washington, the son of a father who had gone to school in England and had several large Virginia estates. Left fatherless at the age of eleven, the boy was shunted between two half brothers and picked up a little irregular schooling in the intervals of learning how to raise tobacco and stock and manage a plantation. He took to surveying in boyhood and decided that it was to be his profession, one that in those days sent a man roving for weeks on end, improvising his sleeping quarters, shooting wild turkey and chewing it on the bone. In the French and Indian Wars, he had suffered the horrors of Braddock's rout. He had horses shot from under him and went home to Virginia with a local reputation for being at all times unflappable. Then his health failed him, and he resigned his commission.

At the age of twenty-seven he married a very rich widow and settled on a majestic stretch of land, at Mount Vernon overlooking the Potomac. His wife had brought him the pleasant dowry of some profitable real estate, fifteen thousand acres near Williamsburg—what by today's exchange would be about a quarter of a million dollars—and one hundred and fifty slaves, whose condition, he confessed, embarrassed him. But he was an eighteenth-century man, and "emancipation" was a remote and strange doctrine. He assumed he would live out his days as a rich Virginia planter, but then, at the age of forty-three, he received the call.

I suspect most Americans would today be put off by his air of a prosperous landowner and real-estate operator in the guise of a rather down-the-nose British colonel. His most idolatrous biographers have been unable to find much evidence of charm, or even jollity, in him. He was imperious, massively self-sufficient, and he had decided ideas about the relations of rank and rank, class and class. He did not, for instance, like to be touched, and when he became the first President he laid down a rule that people coming to see him should remain standing in his presence. He arrived for his inauguration with a flourish of outriders and he shook no hands. Thomas Jefferson was greatly offended by the color and pomp of this ceremony and thought it "not at all in character with the simplicity of republican governments, and looking—as if wishfully —to those of European courts." As he took the oath, a bystanding Senator whispered to his neighbor: "I fear we may have exchanged George the Third for George the First."

Yet there were several things about him that made him the unquestioned leader of the new nation. A pervasive sense of responsibility, an unflagging impression of shrewd judgment, and total integrity. It can best be summed up in what the drama critics call "presence." But it was nothing rehearsed. It was the presence of nothing but character.

The war was only eighteen months old when it seemed that all was lost. The British captured Philadelphia, and many of the Congress took to the

---

Overleaf: *Beneath a lurid sky, American troops engage the British at Princeton, New Jersey, on January 3, 1777. After an initial reverse, Washington won the battle.*

mountains. They were a frightened and divided body of men—divided between genuine revolutionaries and sunshine patriots, between dedicated colonial statesmen and secret Loyalists, and a clutter of money grubbers selling arms or commissions, or merchants whose anxious interest was to see that Spain got the lands beyond the Appalachians so that trade would not go West. The word got to a delirious London that Washington was trapped in a frigid valley, and that the war was over. The first part was correct—but not the second.

In the bleakest winter, of 1777–1778, Washington was camped in Valley Forge, about twenty miles northwest of Philadelphia. He picked it for obvious military advantages. It lay between a creek and a broad river, and the hills were high enough to survey the main supply routes from the South into New England and the roads from Philadelphia that led to the gunneries and powder mills of the interior. He refused to go inland and leave the fertile Pennsylvania farming country as a granary for the enemy. He refused also to commandeer the villages, which hadn't enough food for the swarms of refugees from Philadelphia. So he chose this bare place, and his eleven thousand men built their tents with timber from the neighboring woods.

In the beginning life was bearable, even agreeable. The men were snug in their new huts, the generalissimo moved into a solid farmhouse. Mrs. Washington came to stay, so did some of the officers' wives. There were cheerful dinner parties and no lack of food and wine. But the party was short-lived. The winter snows came early, and by January there were oceans of mud. Congress wouldn't, or couldn't, commission supplies and told Washington to plunder the nearest farmers, which he refused to do. When the main stores ran low, the men started to forage for hickory nuts and the more edible local fauna. By March—when the countryside was blasted by blizzards—a third of them were down with typhus or smallpox and, of course, dysentery. Medical services barely existed, and the besieged army began to thin out alarmingly, if not from disease and actual starvation, then from desertion. Half of the living had neither shoes nor shirts. In the end, Washington was left with something over three thousand men, technically able-bodied, actually half starving.

To this implacable man the ordeal was grim but quite simple. Being an eighteenth-century gentleman-soldier with a puritan core meant that when the chips were down all the agreeable things of life—parties, good food, comfort, professional dignity—were baubles. The winds whistled and the food gave out and the fields stank with death and disease, and Washington's life simplified itself into one hard principle—duty. He had given his word that he would hold on with his army, however sick and bedraggled it might be, and he proceeded to do so. The spring came in and epidemic sickness flourished. But then the French formally entered

Probably the least-known life portrait of George Washington, this heroic painting by John Trumbull shows the general at Verplanck's Point on the Hudson in 1782. Finished in 1790, it was based on sketches Trumbull made on the scene earlier.

Retreating toward Valley Forge in the autumn of 1777, Washington made an abortive attack on the main British camp at Germantown (above). Later, in a night-time skirmish at Paoli (right), British troops surprised the sleeping Continentals.

Commons for the repeal of the Stamp Act; next day to sail for France to run up for the King a report on Mesmer and animal magnetism; that night to write a love letter to Madame Helvetius. The mold has been lost of this American eighteenth-century archetype, the domesticated and urbane Leonardo da Vinci who finds no knowledge odd, the very opposite of a highbrow or trendy intellectual, for he was a man with the widest range of interests who had no preconceived hierarchy of their relative value.

He had one heavy quality. With systematic piety, he ticked off, on a specially prepared calendar, the virtues he would practice on assigned days of the week. Luckily, however, he was a happy hypocrite and his good intentions were cheerfully defeated by the pricking of the flesh. He might talk up the value of abstemiousness, but he advised all young sons to take old women for mistresses because "they are more discreet . . . and so grateful."

He was so much the most familiar American in England that the cagey Staffordshire potters made a figure of him and sold it under three titles: B. Franklin, G. Washington (nobody knew what *he* looked like), and Old English Country Gentleman.

What makes him, after two centuries, not merely impressive but lovable is his absolute lack of arrogance and the steady goodness of his belief that in helping to create the American Republic he was founding a truer order of society. Once, when he came home, he opened a package and found that his wife had ordered some silver knives from London. He retired to his journal and sighed: "Alas, it is by luxury and the vanity of women that empires decay."

The other invaluable ideologue of the Revolution, almost forty years Franklin's junior, was Thomas Jefferson, that thirty-three-year-old Virginia lawyer-squire who was in the main responsible for writing the birth certificate of the United States of America, the Declaration of Independence.

It was worked out in Philadelphia by a committee of five, in a stuffy room over a stable plagued by horseflies, in the hot early summer of 1776, and adopted, in all its clauses except two, by a vote of twelve of the colonies now become states (New York waited awhile). The new "Congress," like most revolutionary governments, preferred to blame the rulers of the parent country and not its people, and a brave denunciation of slavery was deleted at the insistence of Southern owners and Northern shippers. It was published "to a candid world" on July 2 but dated on July 4. The signatures—fifty-six in all—came later.

The first signature, which is almost as large as that of a motion picture star, is that of a man from Massachusetts, John Hancock, who escaped capture by the British in the first battle of the War of Independence and then had his ship confiscated and burned. He wrote his signature in such a way, he said, that "the King of England can read it without his glasses." This whimsical act alone made him immortal, for an American handing out a contract for signature is apt to ask for "your John Hancock." After Hancock, the Declaration was signed by four of the five who drafted it (the fifth—Robert Livingston, an imposing owner of iron mines, being absent in New York): Franklin; John Adams, a Massachusetts lawyer who was to become the second President of the United States; the thirty-three-year-old Thomas Jefferson, who wrote out the final draft; and Roger Sherman of Connecticut, a lawyer who had started out as an apprentice shoemaker and whose habit of picking his teeth during the drafting sessions so provoked Franklin that he threatened the retaliation of "playing my harmonica."

Let us glance at some of the other revolutionaries who signed then or later. Philip Livingston, a New York merchant who organized the ban on importing British goods and who was in private "a breaker of hearts." Thomas Nelson, a Virginia planter, who gave the order to his own soldiers to blow up his splendid house as the British commander approached to occupy it. Charles Carroll of Maryland, an Irish-American Catholic squire, lawyer, and businessman who had the foresight to invest early on in such novelties as canal companies and railroads; he outlived all the other signers and died, at the age of ninety-five, the wealthiest man in America. Benjamin Rush, a Pennsylvania doctor, eminent in America and Europe as the pioneer of what we call psychiatry. John Witherspoon, a Scottish clergyman immigrant, the first president of what is today Princeton University, who was more American than the Americans except in his almost fanatical loathing of what he was the first man to dub "Americanisms." William Floyd, a New York landowner, whose house and extensive grounds are now the site of a nuclear research station; he was immortalized rather late in life—in death—by a motor expressway named after him on Long Island. And Jefferson's teacher and idol, George Wythe, the most eminent professor of law in the colonies, a rich man who died a little before his time had come (he was said to have been poisoned by his nephew, later charitably described as "an impatient heir"). The rest of the signers were a variety of lawyers, shippers, merchants, planters, who would not strike us today as revolutionary types.

But then, in the late eighteenth century, the idea of revolution itself was quite new, and neither its forms nor its practitioners could be recognized on sight. It was hardly possible for enlightened men in England, the heirs of a confident philosophy of universal order, to grasp the new shapes of society fashioned by "the American, this new man" or to feel the imminence of a radical break with their own forms of government. Alexander Pope had crystallized the general prejudice about government in a droll couplet: "For *forms* of government let fools contest, Whate'er is best *administered* is best." Like the Republicans of the early 1930s contemplating the ruins of the Coolidge-Hoover prosperity, the English felt that something must have gone wrong with "management," but that it could always be fixed. So the very prospect of a violent, let alone a successful, revolution was remote until it came hurtling into view. Furthermore, the men who defended the American revolt in the House of Commons did so on the wrong grounds. Very few, if any, of them sensed that two sentences written by Jefferson into the Declaration would shake the ordered world of their century.

The first was: ". . . that all Men are created equal, that they are endowed by their Creator with certain unalienable rights, that among these are Life, Liberty and the pursuit of Happiness." There was a lot of argument among the states over that phrase. And in the end many of the men who signed the Declaration, while letting "happiness" stand as a no doubt worthy general aim, went home and wrote into their separate state constitutions "life, liberty, and the acquisition and protection of property." This was not merely a tycoon's reflex. To most of them property was no dowry. It was the means of life they, or their fathers or grandfathers, had been forced to wrench out of a wilderness.

The second sentence was the stick of dynamite. Everybody knows it now, and at high school commencement exercises it is throbbingly recited as a noble, but self-evident, proposition. Yet it took a century or so for an Englishman (to be more accurate, a Scot—Lord Acton) to recognize in this one sentence the flame of a quite new revolutionary doctrine: ". . . that to secure these rights, Governments are instituted among Men, *deriving their just powers from the consent of the governed.*"

Let us forget for the moment (what we make a habit of forgetting today) the implication that there may be unjust powers—responding to the injustice of life itself—in which the governed have no say. But the idea that if you felt you were being unjustly governed, you—you being the butcher, the baker, the candlestick maker—had some "right" to resist or overthrow the government: this was a firebrand that was to blow up France and the German republic and imperial Russia and eventually the whole idea of empire. We have come to accept this right, and, looking back over revolutions from the Peasants' Revolt to the latest South American coup, we can make one fairly certain generalization about the cause of revolutions: when the people in power can neither keep the consent of the governed nor keep *down* the dissent of the governed, then there will be a blowup.

Mass-produced in Staffordshire, this pottery figure was available labeled "B. Franklin" or "Old English Country Gentleman."

Gᵈ Washington

4

INVENTING
A NATION

William Ewart Gladstone, a consummate politician and the patriarch of British prime ministers, called the Constitution of the United States "the most wonderful work ever struck off at a given time by the brain and purpose of man." Whose was the brain? And what was the purpose?

The brains were undoubtedly those of the colonial Establishment, yet these men varied greatly from state to state—being Quakers or free-thinkers or yeoman farmers in Pennsylvania, Congregational divines in Massachusetts, Anglican lawyers and landowners in Virginia, heathen shippers and merchants in New York, and so on. We should also remember that it was comparatively easier in the eighteenth century for a man of energy and talent, or energy and cunning, to "establish" himself than in the great era of the industrial wage slave.

Their purpose was to invent a national government that would still leave the states with the sovereign powers they had grown used to. A laudable aim that proved, as we shall see, to be a practical impossibility.

The Revolutionary War did not end quite so summarily as we might gather from the pictures of Lord Cornwallis, the British commander, surrendering his sword at Yorktown on October 19, 1781. George III, for one, turned a blind eye on such a scene, simply finding it incredible that His Majesty's crack forces should have been defeated by the American "rabble" and that the thirteen prosperous if cantankerous colonies were lost forever. The American defeat coincided with his final failure to rule both the executive and legislative branches of the government at home, the last tenacious effort of a British monarch to rule both Parliament and people. He actually drew up two drafts of an instrument of abdication, in which he made no excuses and frankly admitted that "this patriotic endeavor [at royal rule] has proved unsuccessful." After that he made one or two fitful raids on the parliamentary power but then slipped, with remarkable sportsmanship, into an acceptance of his shrunken role. And when the colonies at last achieved their indepen-

With scarlet coats and freshly pipe-clayed straps gleaming, British troops march out of their defenses and lay down their arms after surrendering at Yorktown. Flanking the route were files of French soldiers (rear) and Americans. The British bands played "The World Turned Upside Down."

dence and sent over John Adams as the first American Minister to the Court of Saint James's, George III made the magnanimous concession to Adams's face: "I will be very frank with you. I was the last to consent to the separation: but the separation having been made, and having become inevitable, I have always said, as I say now, that I would be the first to meet the friendship of the United States as an independent power."

However, after the official surrender, the British still held New York. They also held, though loosely, some Southern ports and garrisons, as well as outposts in the wilderness above Ohio. But these were all doomed to yield, and in 1783 a peace treaty was signed at Paris. The British brought some bargaining strength to the table, since they had won brilliant naval victories in the West Indies and they held New York till the end. Obviously, though, they had to grant the total independence of the new nation called the United States of America. They yielded up therefore all the lands between Canada and Florida, as well as the disputed lands between the Mississippi and the Appalachians, but retained a share of the Newfoundland fisheries and navigation rights along the whole Mississippi.

For their part, the French hoped for a while to limit the expansion of the new nation by having both banks of the Mississippi and the whole lower valley transferred to Spain. In any event, they were satisfied to see the British stripped of her colonies, leaving a small, disheveled nation on a huge continent at the mercy of French protection. Spain wanted rewards far beyond her prowess as a fighting ally; she wrangled for Gibraltar and settled for Florida instead.

But now the peace conference was bedeviled by a word that haunts the defeated in every civil war: "reprisal." What was going to happen to the losers who lived on the old battleground, to the one third of a nation that had fought with the British or stayed suspiciously neutral or were known to have had a Loyalist brother or cousin or whoever? The treaty had expressed humane promises about compensation for seized lands and houses and other possessions. But the Congress was an infant with no authority to see that this was done, and the treatment of the Loyalists varied alarmingly from state to state.

The Pennsylvania Quakers, most of whom had refused to fight at all on principle, were understandably compassionate. South Carolina, considering that the British had dealt miserably during the war with many of her citizens on prison ships, was surprisingly generous. A stout, rebel New Yorker, on the other hand, writing to Alexander Hamilton in the middle of the war, boasted that "the spirit of the Tories, we have great reason to believe, is entirely broken in this state . . . I wish the several states would follow our example. Pennsylvania, in particular, would experience many good effects from a vigorous manly execution." Indeed, in most of the states the Loyalists had a brutal time. They lost their houses and businesses. They had no legal redress from assault and slander. They had to pay for the damage done by mobs to their homes. And in two states they were required to pay double and treble taxes. A protest against the riding of Loyalists on rails brought from George Washington the bland thought that to stop this quaint custom would be an interference with the liberty of the people!

At last they were forced into exile in great numbers—to Canada, to the West Indies, or back to England. A hundred ships sailed out of Charleston jammed with Loyalists. The British commander at New York (whose troops set fire to the city before they embarked) was so fearful of mob reprisals that he refused to give up the port until the last refugee was aboard. One of them made the forlorn note in his diary: "There will scarcely be a village in England without some American dust in it by the time we are all at rest."

I suppose you could say that it was bound to happen. The war had ended in a blaze of patriotism, and the people were so peacock proud that sooner or later the demagogues and the mob between them might well have menaced the lives of a population of "renegades." So, for a brief and heady time the patriots reveled in the fiction proclaimed by the revolutionary leaders, of a brave and indissoluble alliance of new states. Even so level-headed a man as John Adams wrote:

The second day of July, 1776, will be the most memorable epoch in the history of America. It ought to be commemorated as the day of deliverance, by solemn acts of devotion to God Almighty. It ought to be solemnized with pomp and parade, with shows, games, sports, guns, bells, bonfires and illuminations from one end of this continent to the other, from this time forward, for evermore.

But, as so many new African states discovered in the ecstasy of "Uhuru!," there is a morning after. Once the war and the celebrations were over, the indissoluble union began to dissolve. Like the victims of a hurricane or a blitz, the old colonists had learned that there is no livelier stimulus to brotherhood than physical danger. But once the storm had passed, they headed for home and went their own ways. They were drunk on the pride of their sovereignty, but not as Americans: as New Yorkers, Georgians, Marylanders, Vermonters—and so much so that they began to act like independent nations. The states hemmed in by other states were frantic to stake claims to the unsettled lands in the West. They developed their own money systems and levied their own

---

Overleaf: *Many Loyalists fled to Britain and made claims for their wartime losses. An inset in the portrait of Judge John Wilmot shows them being welcomed.*

chief executive, a lifetime senate recruited only from men of property, a central government that could absolutely veto the laws of the states. Indeed, he advocated—without much hope of success—extinguishing the states altogether.

At the opposite pole from Hamilton was a Virginian twice his age, a wealthy landowner with distinguished military and statesmanlike forebears who you would expect to have been an automatic seconder of Hamilton's ideas. He was George Mason, sixty-two years old, an uncompromising democrat about half a century before his time. He had organized the Ohio Company, whose surveys in western Pennsylvania brought on the French and Indian Wars. He was a prominent member of Virginia's "insubordinate" House of Burgesses and a Raleigh Tavern radical. He had drawn up the Virginia Bill of Rights, which went to the heart of the liberties the British had abused: searching without warrant, trying people twice for the same crime, suppressing free assembly. He called himself a radical republican and argued long, and fruitlessly, to have these assaults on individual liberty prohibited in the text of the Constitution. He argued to the end in favor of the weakest possible central government consonant with a confederacy. But since this was what most delegates believed they had tried and found wanting, he was beaten all along the line. So he concentrated on the rights of individuals, and argued for the inclusion of a bill of rights, and didn't get it.

Figuratively sitting in between these two was James Madison, an undramatic scholar, thirty-six years old, also from Virginia. A man destined at one time for the ministry, a Hebrew scholar apparently so innocent of practical politics that he was defeated for reelection to the Virginia Convention because he recoiled from the vulgar necessity of stoking the electors with the usual ration of rum. He was eventually elected to the Continental Congress, and when the war was over he went back to Virginia to study law and drum up on the side a campaign to prohibit a general tax for the support of any established religion.

Madison had thought about the defects of the Articles more profoundly than anyone present, and had already explored the perils of other confederacies. When he arrived in Philadelphia, he had with him an outline for a new system. It provided the groundwork for the so-called Virginia plan, which became the substance of the long debate. Its main point, which Madison was ready to illustrate to a fare-thee-well, was that you could never reconcile the sovereignty of each state with an "aggregate sovereignty" simply called a republic. He appeared armed with a study of confederacies ancient and modern, and he lectured the delegates at great length to prove that no confederacy had ever succeeded that set up a conflict of authority between the national and provincial governments. The main purpose of government, whether local or national, was "to act upon and for the individual citizen"—a new and vital concept. Another which enlarged a concern for "the individual citizen" to the protection of minorities was his awareness that a democratically elected government can encourage the majority to ride roughshod over the minority.

More than any other of the active debaters, Madison seized the principle that made the American Constitution durable; more than any other, he had the instinct of the balance valve, which yields steam protectively first to one side, then the other. His ideals were very well tempered by his survey of other systems and by a skeptical view of human nature. "If men were virtuous," he once reminded the Convention, "there would be no need of governments at all." He practically foresaw the rise of political parties as an inevitable exercise of human nature. Tactfully avoiding Washington's characterization of "associations and combinations," he maintained that you could not, and should not, try to suppress "factions," for they expressed the natural instinct for disagreement, and so were an expression of liberty. The trick would be to keep any one faction from becoming a tyrannous majority. And the way to do that was to leave as many powers as possible to the states and yet to have the national Congress represent all the variety of men, and interests, and factions in the whole country itself. In this willingness to admit the vast and often warring variety of state interests, Madison recognized the value of the "sectionalism" that to this day remains the root and branch of American politics. It has produced such uneasy coalitions as the modern Democratic party, which, considered as a national political party pretending to a single ideology, must often look like an impostor. But the freedom given to sectional interests within it— and within the Republican party, too—does prevent the national legislature from becoming the servant of any single ideology or "faction."

This system would guarantee a balance, however stormy, between national parties, or interests, inside the states. But suppose all the various interests, suppose even that the executive, the legislature, and the judiciary succumbed to the appeal of one powerful interest—the bankers, the farmers, the warmongers, say—what then? This hazard led Madison to the profound discovery that if the separate branches of government were made responsible to *separate constituencies*, then they would always tend to collide. This notion that collision is not only natural to governments but the source of their health was shocking to many of the idealists around him. But when he was challenged to say if the frailties of human nature were the proper elements of good government, he resoundingly replied that he knew no other: "Ambition must be made to counteract ambition. The interest of the man must be connected with the constitutional rights of the place."

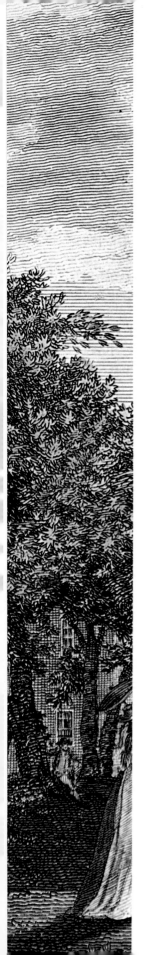

As this central principle was worked out in the setting up of the new government, it became clear that, in Madison's view, both Hamilton and Mason were wrong. Give too much power to the provinces and they will swamp the central government (it had happened). Give to the national government the power to use force on a recalcitrant state, and you invite civil war. So there followed the triumphant theory that dictated the practicable balance of state and national powers: the national government shall not coerce the states or be their rival. Both exist to protect the American citizen.

So the men of Philadelphia boosted the pride, and the sense of reponsibility, of the little states by giving them equal representation in an upper house, the Senate; and they acknowledged the local interests of all the regions by giving them the widest representation—for a shorter term—in the lower house, the House of Representatives. And whatever powers were not stipulated in the Constitution were left to the states: they were to retain, as they do, the control of their own highways, education, banking, taxation, divorce, liquor laws, their own civil and criminal codes. It was a daring thing not to try and reduce the powers of the states. But to do so would have imperiled the whole Constitution by sending the delegates home in a huff. The states were allowed, as they had to be, to diffuse the opportunity for self-government, as also, we ought to add, for corruption.

It sounds like a shattering defeat for Alexander Hamilton, and so it was. When the Convention was all over, he confessed that "no man's ideas are more remote from the plan than my own are known to be." But he added, without a grudge, "Is it possible to deliberate between anarchy and convulsion on one side, and the chance of good to be expected on the other?" Hamilton had the pride of a Roman, and some Roman vices, too—arrogance, a prejudice in favor of men of property, an incurable distaste for "the mob." But he had also a great Roman virtue, that of magnanimity. He did not complain or recriminate because he had lost. To me Hamilton—not a fashionable figure in our day—represents the politician at his very best showing an absence of malice, "a steady willingness," in Mencken's phrase, "to believe that his opponent is as honorable a man as himself, and may be right." He swallowed his most passionate convictions and wrote more than forty brilliant proselytizing essays urging the states to ratify the Constitution. It was a close thing in some states. Virginia, for instance, voted 89 for, 79 against. George Mason and Patrick Henry voted against.

But in the end it was done. After seventeen weeks the weary fifty-five

What we now know as Independence Hall was the Pennsylvania State House when the Constitutional Convention met there in 1787. It looked like this about ten years later.

V. No person shall be held to answer for a capital, or otherwise infamous crime, unless on a presentment or indictment of a Grand Jury, except in cases arising in the land or naval forces, or in the Militia, when in actual service in time of War or public danger; nor shall any person be subject for the same offence to be twice put in jeopardy of life or limb; nor shall be compelled in any criminal case to be a witness against himself, nor be deprived of life, liberty, or property, without due process of law; nor shall private property be taken for public use, without just compensation.

VI. In all criminal prosecutions, the accused shall enjoy the right to a speedy and public trial, by an impartial jury of the State and district wherein the crime shall have been committed, which district shall have been previously ascertained by law, and to be informed of the nature and cause of the accusation; to be confronted with the witnesses against him; to have compulsory process for obtaining witnesses in his favor, and to have the Assistance of Counsel for his defence.

VII. In Suits at common law, where the value in controversy shall exceed twenty dollars, the right of trial by jury shall be preserved, and no fact tried by a jury shall be otherwise re-examined in any Court of the United States, than according to the rules of the common law.

VIII. Excessive bail shall not be required, nor excessive fines imposed, nor cruel and unusual punishments inflicted.

IX. The enumeration in the Constitution of certain rights shall not be construed to deny or disparage others retained by the people.

X. The powers not delegated to the United States by the Constitution, or prohibited by it to the States, are reserved to the States respectively, or to the people.

It would not be a bad idea, and would save us from the spouting of much florid and impractical rhetoric, if a President were required on the day of his inauguration, not to make a speech, but to stand before the Chief Justice of the United States and recite the Bill of Rights. For most of the decent, and indeed the preposterous, claims to constitutional liberties that come up before the Supreme Court in our day are alleged violations of the Bill of Rights. The astuteness of including the Ninth Amendment has been proved elaborately down the centuries by the fact that sixteen other amendments have been added, and there will be more; for the persistence of men and institutions in tinkering with liberties we take for granted is unending.

Jefferson's incessant anxiety for the individual as against the states was certainly quickened by his living in France during the whole five years up to the brink of the French Revolution. But it was rooted in his memories of life in Virginia, which at a distance of three thousand miles wove in his mind a fantasy model of a prosperous republic inhabited by "God's finest creation"—the farmers. You might think of such a man, who disliked cities and idolized farmers, as a simple, rural, sentimental crank. On the contrary, he was a remarkable American eighteenth-century type, an upper-class, classless, inventive, scholarly, eccentric country squire. His house, Monticello, near Charlottesville in Virginia, was built to his own design, and it reflects, more than the elegant homes of most statesmen, the charm and the idiosyncrasy of his interests and his passions. He anticipated Le Corbusier by more than a century and a half by turning his house into "a machine for living," except that Jefferson's view of life and living made certain that it was never less than a home as well. Throughout the house we come on novelties of his invention: a twenty-four-hour clock; a revolving chair, in which he could move with the light always over his shoulder; a four-sided lectern that allowed a chamber-music quartet to play from the same stand. Jefferson designed his own furnishings, his own spectacles, his own medicine chest. He was an amateur of everything—of music, astronomy and meteorology, of architecture, anthropology, and gardening. He cultivated the famous Albemarle pippin, which—if anyone cares—was Queen Victoria's favorite apple.

He was a lifelong journal jotter and notetaker. He wrote reams of notes on the Greek and Roman authors, on contemporary French philosophers, on geology, on Hebrew manuscripts, most famously on his native state of Virginia, a curiously intense bit of writing that brings the same concern to bear on the varieties of trees, plants, and wildflowers in the state as on the locations of the known Indian tribes and the white's relations with his slaves. He also had a theory of currency, which he carried with the Congress against the bankers, and so became known as "the father of the dollar." His objections to the laboriousness of pounds, shillings, and pence anticipated by two hundred years the wisdom of the British government: the ordinary man or woman "is used to be puzzled by adding the farthings, taking out the twenties and carrying them on; but when he came to pounds, where he had only tens to carry forward, it was easy and free from error." He suggested that, since "everyone knows the facility of decimal arithmetic," it should be adopted in the coinage "to the great ease of the community."

If there is one notebook I'd give a great deal to have in the original, it's the one he carried around Europe, methodically putting down all the detestable things a republic must not have. "No public statues," a prejudice the American people have successfully overcome. No "titles of nobility . . . a very great vanity . . . which tends to prolong the artificial aristocracy of birth and wealth as against the natural aristocracy of talent and virtue." He went to London and visited the courts: no wigs on

judges. "We must not have men sitting in judgment who look like mice peeping out of oakum."

There is something comical, and maybe a little prim, about the earnestness of all this, but something, too, straightforwardly innocent in an age of powerful intrigue and far-ranging cynicism. He was shocked to hear of the Constitutional Convention's rule of secrecy and wrote at once to John Adams to deplore "so abominable a precedent." Jefferson seems to have had none of Madison's fear for the tyranny of majority opinion. Let everything come out, and the judgment of the common people will be sound. Over and over again, he writes of the essential "goodness and wisdom" of the common people. It forces us to wonder how many common people he knew, outside of the friendly farmers and the obedient servants and slaves who ministered to his serenity in his beloved Monticello. He disliked the hubbub of Washington, a place he called "that Indian swamp in the wilderness," and retreated as often as possible to the Blue Ridge and its systematic chores and pleasures. Until his old age, when he saw a disaster brewing between the slave states and the free states, and when he came to fear, of all things, the power of "the federal judiciary," he pictured life in America as a long pastoral symphony, a continuing Utopia of chivalrous and learned rulers walking hand in hand with good, honest farmers in—a favorite phrase—"perfect harmony."

Alexander Hamilton groaned to hear him. Three years before his death, Hamilton wrote: "Every day proves to me more and more that this American world is not for me." Maybe Hamilton could see a little farther into the future than Jefferson. He understood that the original mold of the Union, a civilized federation of states planted along the Eastern seaboard, had been broken. He saw over the mountains, where an unlettered generation of hunters, trappers, farmers, and their broods were hacking and sometimes slaughtering their way into rude settlements. These people had few, if any, links with the writers of the Constitution, and they would transform the Republic beyond the imagining of the learned men, the city-shrewd men, the paternal squirearchy of the eighteenth century. By 1804, the year Hamilton died, the French and the Spanish had yielded up the Mississippi Valley and the infinite lands beyond to the Anglo-Saxon mountaineers and frontiersmen. It was a prospect that ravished Jefferson and threw Hamilton into despair. "Democracy," he wrote, two days before he died, "is our real disease."

Every inch the young diplomat, Thomas Jefferson was painted by Mather Brown in London in 1786, shortly before he succeeded Benjamin Franklin as American envoy to the French court.

5
GONE WEST

Where the West begins is a question that has puzzled foreigners, immigrants, and Easterners for centuries. It has been answered for most of us by an emblem, by the stark appearance on the horizon of a one-street town that the movies have made into a stereotype. As late as the Second World War, it was possible to come on the genuine article at hundred-mile intervals through Arizona and Nevada and in the western foothills of the Sierras: a short row of wooden false fronts—a hardware store, a raddled saloon, the shell of the United States post office, the ghost of a newspaper office—standing alone under an encircling sky at the end of a dirt road that led nowhere.

Today the true ghost towns have been done over, with much facetiousness, by way of lurid saloon signs and synthetic gambling joints, as tourist traps; or they have been overlaid by the neat clutter of suburbia; or they have sunk without trace. There is one in Southern California—Bodie, eight thousand feet up in the Sierras—that the state has fenced off against "development" and disaster. Thus protected, it still remains a vivid memorial to the West of a century ago. The wooden false fronts are weathered into a coppery brown. They lean at threatening angles over a high boardwalk on a rambling dirt street that is sometimes as hard as cement and sometimes squelching with mud from the tumbling mountain rains. Drills, picks, and wagon wheels lie rusting in stubble grass below the old mine and mill up on the mountain, and inside the stores can be found the moldering domestic relics—the crockery, coins, wedding licenses, lanterns, rocking chairs, stoves—of a century ago. Bodie—a misspelling of one W. S. Body who found gold there in 1859—struck it rich in 1876. For four years the place was roaring with life and death: one killing a day, fifty-six saloons and gambling joints, twelve thousand people brimming with sap and mischief and vice. By 1883 it was mostly abandoned, and in 1932 a fire browned it off. Today, it is a graveyard up among the rolling cumulus clouds. It is as forgotten and forlorn as the Plains of Troy. But it is unforgettably what we all like

Vast herds of buffalo—more properly bison—were one of the glories of the Great Plains. The Indians, as in this 1840 painting by A. J. Miller, killed them for food and hides. But with the coming of the white man the slaughter increased radically, and by the end of the century only two wild herds were left between the Atlantic and the Pacific.

155

to think of as the West. Because the West is always a stretch of particular landscape, beginning with the eastern rise of the Rockies and going through to the Pacific. And it is also a state of mind: the idea still of El Dorado, of getting away from it all, of leading a new and luckier life under that "big sky," of being—as the song says—"bound for the Promised Land."

But where the West begins depends when you asked the question. In the nineteenth century Charles Dickens got no farther than St. Louis, nine hundred miles short even of the Rockies. He went home convinced he had seen the West, and he declared it to be a fraud. In the seventeenth century the West began practically at the Atlantic seashore. It was synonymous with "the frontier," that inland danger line where the colonial settlement ended and the woods and the Indians started. In the coastal towns of Massachusetts, a fond father, seeing his daughter off on a journey of only fifteen miles to visit relatives in another settlement, wrote in his diary: "I did greatly fear for Abigail's safety, as she is gone into Duxbury. It is her first journey into the West, and I shall pray mightily for her early return."

In the time of Jefferson and Hamilton, the West was anywhere beyond the crest of the Appalachians. Hunters and scouts had nosed along the eastern ridges for decades, searching, in this dense haystack of mountain and forest, for the needle of a trail. It was found in 1750 by an Englishman who had gone out as an agent for a Virginia land company. Thomas Walker, a doctor, found a gap, at 1,665 feet, on the border of what are today the states of Kentucky, Tennessee, and Virginia. It was a natural gap beyond which the Indians had beaten out, to the south and west, a great system of trails. Dr. Walker, a loyal Tory, named it after the Duke of Cumberland, but it was left to a veteran of the French and Indian Wars named Daniel Boone to make it a highway into the promised land so many of his brothers in arms had glimpsed, and then had forbidden to them.

Boone was a Pennsylvanian who had been a wagoner in Braddock's ill-fated expedition against the French at Fort Duquesne. After the war he started roaming, first into Florida and then into "the West." If it was the ideas of such as Jefferson that invented the new nation, it was the hardihood of such as Boone that shaped and secured it. He was an undefeatable hunter, explorer, and surveyor for several land companies, and he deserves the title of the first Westerner.

Buried in the shady cleft of an overhanging slab of rock in the Great Smoky Mountains there is a hut, built of split timber, that is about eight feet wide and four feet high. It would serve as a rather cramped kennel for a mastiff, but it has, in fact, been lately authenticated as a hideaway of

In 1820, the year of his death, Daniel Boone was a tough and soured old man. His brave days of exploration were long since over, he had lost title to most of the land he claimed, and he was living in a cabin in Missouri when an itinerant artist named Chester Harding made the long journey into the backwoods to paint this portrait.

Daniel Boone. In places like this, Boone would rest awhile before going out by day into the mountains, living the essentially stealthy and self-sufficient life of a rover—hunting, trapping, camping, surveying, killing an Indian scout when need be, surveying, and resting again. He disappeared for as long as two years at a stretch. Some men, some with whole companies, disappeared altogether. No wonder the phrase "gone West" became a synonym for death, a meaning it retained in England throughout the First World War. (I remember being puzzled, as a small boy, to be told that an uncle had been killed in France and then to hear the grown-ups saying that most of his pals had "gone West," too.)

Boone tried again and again to beat a westward trail into a new colony, into the rolling, open country of Kentucky. Before he made it he had been "adopted" by an Indian tribe and escaped; he had seen a brother killed and families massacred; he nearly died in a blizzard, and another time came close to drowning. At the end he was swindled out of the tracts of land he cleared and laid title to. But, in March 1775, following the plan and direction of one Judge Richard Henderson, the president of the Transylvania Company, Boone started from eastern Tennessee with thirty woodsmen to clear a road west that families of pioneers might safely use. They went through the narrow Cumberland Gap, picked up woodland paths, joined trails beaten down by wandering bison, skirted Indian encampments, rolled away rocks, and hacked down forest and brush and posted guide markers at difficult sites.

This so-called Wilderness Road was nearly three hundred miles long and ended at the Ohio River at Louisville. It would be another twenty years before it was graded so it would be fit for wagons. But Boone's grinding, Herculean feat of trail-blazing was glorified in ballads and tall tales. It enticed over one hundred thousand people to go into the new territories of western Tennessee and Kentucky within fifteen years. Thirty years after them, by 1820, the population of the United States had doubled, and the overflow of the native young and new arrivals from Europe made the Cumberland Gap the main Southern highway to the West, as it is today in the form of a six-lane Interstate.

They were mostly unlettered folk, hunters, disappointed farmers from Europe or the East, trappers, old army scouts, French and Indian Wars veterans still unadjusted to home and hearth, the adventurous, the tough, the footloose, and—we must believe—a nucleus of sturdy and honorable men who took along with them Daniel Boone's three essentials:"A good gun, a good horse, and a good wife." They needed also good health, good luck, and an ax. And one other thing—salt.

Salt was the only preservative for the traveler's food. Before the Revolution salt had to be shipped at great price from the West Indies. The first pioneers carried it laboriously over the mountains by pack

Leading his pack horse, a traveler picks his way through the first rocky pass on the extreme eastern edge of the Appalachians. From this point, northwest of Philadelphia, trails led in a southwesterly direction along the lines of the mountain ridges, finally breaking through into Kentucky and Tennessee at the Cumberland Gap.

UNDER ☆ MY☆ ☆ WINGS ☆

In 1803, the year of the Louisiana Purchase, Boqueto de Woieseri painted this
patriotic view of New Orleans. It is now in the Chicago Historical Society collection.

of the Carolinas, on soil so poor that his father took two years to raise a crop and died of exhaustion at twenty-nine, when Andrew was two years old. He was only eight when the Revolution broke out, and in his early teens the British descended on the Waxhaws to burn and pillage. At thirteen he was a soldier, fought and was captured in a skirmish, and was scarred for life by a saber blow from a British officer. He was put with his brother in a prisoners' stockade, got smallpox, and within the year lost both his brothers and his mother. She had been a nurse to the Carolinians kept on British prison ships, had come home with tales of brutality and neglect, and herself died of "ship fever," cholera. At fourteen, he was alone in the world. He studied law and in time became a county judge, but much of his life was spent protecting the new settlements in Mississippi and Florida from Indian attacks, and in patrolling the settlers' trails through to the West, tramping in silence "for two days and nights, never daring to shoot game or kindle a fire," and resting always back to back, with a rifle cocked. When he commanded expeditions against the Indian tribes of the South, his natural suspicion and distrust of the red men was inflamed by finding, on the captured rifles that had killed his men, the imprint of British manufacturers. The subtle, strong alliance between the British and the Indians in the short War of 1812 galvanized his native belligerence. A cunning and brave soldier, an impetuous man (he was wounded twice in duels and killed a man in another), by the time he had helped win the war of 1812 he had come to suspect all Easterners, to distrust all bankers, to hate the British, and to loathe George Washington.

The great Indian ally of the British in 1812 was a Shawnee chief, Tecumseh, and to him the war was by no means the "foolish, unnecessary" war it is called in textbooks. It was the last hope of an Indian confederacy and of their claim to lands in the interior. Before the war Tecumseh had traveled from the Gulf of Mexico to the Great Lakes, pleading for a united Indian nation to make a stand against the white man. The coalition failed in a single battle in 1811, at Tippecanoe in Indiana. After that, the best hope of the Indians lay with the British, and after them there was none.

The white men who manned the (postwar) U.S. Army trading posts gave assurances that the Indians' rights to their own lands were absolute. But those lands kept shrinking as the whites moved westward. When they came into the flat lands beyond the mountains and down into the Mississippi delta they knew what they wanted their West to look like: an empire of cotton, not an Indian camp ground. So in 1830 the great cotton states of Mississippi, Alabama, and Georgia outlawed the tribal kingdoms, and President Jackson pushed a bill through Congress ordering all the Indian tribes, whether farmers or hunters, peaceable or

At the age of 78, shortly before his death, Andrew Jackson became the first President to have his picture taken. The year was 1845 and the daguerrotypist was probably Daniel Adams.

hostile, to move west of the Mississippi. And they started to move away, the Choctaws, the Creeks, and the Chickasaws. There was a brave pause while the Cherokees appealed to the Supreme Court and Chief Justice John Marshall upheld their claim that there was no constitutional right to remove them from their ancestral lands. Jackson called this decision "too preposterous," and, in what is surely one of the most shameless and arbitrary acts of an American President, he simply ignored the Supreme Court and ordered the army to "get them out." And so, in what is truly called "the trail of tears," thirty thousand Cherokees were persuaded or chained, gently led or viciously driven, as far west as Oklahoma, and along the way a quarter of them died.

This imperious ruling came to apply wherever the white man cared to explore. But in what we know as the Far West there were tough tribes whose blessed possession of the horse would enable them to hunt for their food, go on warring among themselves, and put off the day, for another sixty years, when the white man would subdue them all.

In the meantime, the Far West was an exploitable wilderness for the white land pirates who had the stamina to knock around in it. Among them, of course, were roving French-Canadians so remote from any fame or notice in the East that it was not until the 1850s that a new kind of pioneer came on the trails and cutoffs they had blazed. One of the most astonishing accomplishments of these Westerners, isolated by two thousand miles from the trans-Appalachian pioneers, was the creation of an international fur trade that in the first two decades of the nineteenth century drew bales of pelts from the waters of the Columbia and the Snake, the Rockies and the Cascades. They set their traps and they prospered mightily throughout the vast and brutal territory supposedly known only to Lewis and Clark and the native Indians. They stumped across the Plains on foot and into the Rockies for a very practical reason. They went after the beaver, not for himself but for what he could be made into, for by a whimsy of fashion, the beaver hat was the racy headgear in New York, Vienna, London, Boston, Philadelphia, and Paris. Until the silk hat supplanted it, it was at the heart of a roaring business.

The British and the Americans each got into the fur trade after their own peculiar fashion. The British followed a straightforward class system. At the top, management—the English and the Scots, who did the hiring and kept the books. Below them were the canoeists, usually French-Canadians. And below them, the trappers—that is to say, the Indians. (By the way, three different grades of Indian tea were shipped out from England, to accommodate the superior and inferior tastes of these three classes.) The Indians caught the animals and delivered the pelts to the British posts for a dollar a throw. The British then sold them in the international market for ten dollars a throw.

In came the Americans, with no preconceptions about a system or a hierarchy. They set their own traps, paddled their own canoes, and employed the Indians to catch the beasts at three or four times the British wage. So the Indians deserted the British companies in large numbers, running the risk of being sued for breach of contract, a formality pretty difficult to proceed with in that sort of country. Several tribes were actually condemned "for personal disloyalty to the Crown." The Americans, however, didn't give a damn about loyalty or whether an Indian would be corrupted by money. They were happy to pay three times the going price and collar the market.

Though this lucrative trade collapsed in the 1830s, it went on long enough to introduce the forerunner of the American trade fair: the institution of the rendezvous, a regular annual gathering where all the bargaining and the buying were done. In wide pastures at the foot of the mountains, the Indians gathered with their pelts and the buyers came in with axes and kettles and dollars and various seductive trinkets, including whiskey. Gradually the rendezvous gave way to trading posts protected by stockades, but these first Western forts were privately owned. Only much later were some of them bought up for hard cash by the United States Army.

When the beaver trade declined, many of the old trappers and scouts retreated to British Columbia or slogged back to St. Louis to hire themselves out as guides along the Oregon Trail. But the Far West held other tempting prospects for adventurous men, especially within the large confines of northern Mexico. This region, it is easy to forget today, enclosed Texas (until 1835), and Arizona, Nevada, California, and Utah (until 1848). Government in these huge Mexican outposts barely existed except in California, and an ambitious man of any nationality could purchase a land grant and, with sufficient industry and panache, make himself the rough-and-ready lord of all he surveyed.

Such a hopeful seigneur was Johann August Sutter, a roving soldier of fortune of Swiss parentage. After speculative pauses in Missouri and the beaver trade and the shipping business to Hawaii, he undertook to found and rule his own California colony. The Mexican governor gave him forty-nine thousand acres along the Sacramento River on the condition that he would turn it into an impregnable Mexican outpost. The Mexicans had been frightened by the arrival of the Russians in pursuit of the sea otter and by their fortified settlement north of San Francisco. The disappearance of the sea otter and the subsequent order of the Czar to

Overleaf: *In 1837 artist A. J. Miller made this sketch in Fort William (later Fort Laramie), a trading station in what is now eastern Wyoming.*

171

"*Mirage on the Prairie or Traders' Caravan*" *was the title A. J. Miller
gave to his view of a wagon train slowly vanishing into the limitless plains.*

It's fun to cook with buffalo chips,
Take one that's newly born.
If I knew once what I know now,
I'd have gone around the Horn.

Once across the Rockies their spirits picked up again, but not for long. Moving south and west they had ahead of them the rolling desert land of Utah, and once across Utah they had another three hundred and fifty-mile walk following the Humboldt River, which begins in grass and bright, rippling water and ends in the bone-bright wilderness that is now the western reach of the state of Nevada. The desert landscape here constantly unfolds a green horizon, but when you come to it you find a scrubby carpet of creosote and mesquite and cat's-claw, some of it poisonous, all of it arid. And now they came on a phenomenon that most of them had never seen. The Humboldt slowed and turned a yellow milky-green, the sure sign that it was impregnated with alkali. The cattle that drank the water died; the humans boiled it and nevertheless had continuous dysentery.

By this time they had been together for three or four months. It was August and normally one hundred or one hundred and ten degrees in any discoverable shade, and the nerves began to snap. People went mad: one man shot his brother because he could no longer stand the sound of his voice, another man tried to strangle a partner for the crime of twirling a luxuriant mustache. This was, they thought at the time, the nadir of the trek. Certainly, brotherly love gave out.

Something else gave out that the people who knew about it dreaded to mention, and the people who didn't discovered too late. The river itself, foul as it was, dribbled and spread into a fetid marsh and at last dried up under the burning sun. It was something they could not credit. They had never seen rivers that simply evaporated and left a scum.

Beyond the end of the Humboldt was nothing but alkali desert, sixty-five miles without any water at all. They could make it in fifty-two hours. But the parched animals were used to rest at the "nooning." They couldn't let them. They had to push on, and when the animals collapsed they left them to die. One man wrote later that you could not possibly mistake the trail through the Humboldt Desert because it was littered at intervals of only thirty yards or so with rusting shafts, bags of putrid bacon, and the skeletons of mules and oxen and the corpses of humans. Some people died of starvation, of thirst or dysentery, and some people died—of just having had it. They crossed sticks and laid them over the body: "Tom Walmsley, born Yorkshire, died this spot, August 10th, 1849." It occurred to some charitable people who could still muse as they staggered that you couldn't get word back to a man's family that he had died nowhere. So they created place names, and wherever the trail turned or there was a new vista they marked a stick and planted it. And the word got back to Geneva or Glasgow or Philadelphia or Frankfurt that the son had died in Endurance, Nevada. I have an old, yellowing automobile map that still peppers the wilderness of Nevada with such names as Fortitude, Desolation, Last Gasp.

For those who survived the ghastly ordeal of the Humboldt there was the sudden miracle of tumbling water again, and tall shade trees and rising hills. But these blessings were a warning of the last huge hurdle. Some Europeans had never heard of it. They thought the last great mountain range was the Rockies. But rearing up beyond the foothills was the great granite fortress of the High Sierras. The later parties learned well that they must get through the Sierras before early September, when the heavy snows began. They had heard fearful, true anecdotes about impatient companies that had been tipped off to smart shortcuts. Some of these daredevils froze in snow-blocked passes. A train that had refused to break up into manageable teams, a company of four hundred, with a hundred wagons and many cattle and mules, went far south to race across Death Valley. They lost or killed and ate all their animals, wandered for weeks in an ocean of sand and out into scarlet canyons and emerged at last, half crazed and gnawing, as their rescuers recalled, "on poor ox meat but little better than basswood bark, and the marrow in their bones run and looked like corruption."

This was the time when the freewheeling companies no longer scorned the prim precautions of the companies that had kept to a strict military discipline. The Charlestown Company came through unscathed. Like the rest who made it before the snows, they tumbled down the western foothills into deep grass and around the golden buttocks of mountains with live oaks dotted over them as in a medieval tapestry. And they came at last to the American River. They called the last stops Pine Vista, and Cool, and Lotus. But it didn't turn out to be Lotus Land for most. The rich diggings had been seized early on by those California ranchers who were to become the founding families, the "Nobs" of San Francisco. They retired to that shanty town on nine wind-blown sandy hills and replaced its tents with shacks and then, as the gold poured in, with mansions on what is still called Nob Hill.

These were the few who had the luck and the muscle and the guile. Many others were bilked out of their strikes and gladly exchanged a bag of gold dust for a ship's passage home. The rest pounded up and down the river valley hoping to grab a little land and sell it a year later at an inflated price. Or they turned into retailers for the stage-coach line that came down from Oregon with eggs at two dollars apiece. Or they stayed on as artisans and saloon keepers in little villages to which they gave either grim or hilarious names, according to their mood, their luck, or

Bierstadt

Thoroughly rough and ready, with saddle blanket and stirrup covers made of buffalo hide, a mountain man sits his undersized pony as if he'd grown there. This was the sort of man emigrants depended on to guide them through the wild stretches on the way west. He was painted by Albert Bierstadt, probably during a Rocky Mountain expedition in 1858.

their sobriety: Brandy Gulch, Chinese Diggings, Humbug Canyon, Knock'Em Stiff, Rich Bar, and Poverty Hill. Sutter's huge acreage was invaded and his livestock burned when he tried to hold off the invaders. Marshall, like Daniel Boone, was swindled out of every claim. He was intimidated by armed guards posted by the Nobs. And when he went to court, he found the Nobs sitting there as judge and jury. He died in total poverty thirty-seven years after his discovery and was buried within sight of his sawmill. Five years later, the state made belated amends by erecting a statue of him made of bronze.

It is a tremendous story. It took courage, or stark insensibility, to walk two thousand miles across the empty continent. But historically it was a freak. The forty-niners were what you might well call "sudden adventurers." Their aim was not to settle Mr. Jefferson's open West. They looked on the American continent as a vast intermediate nuisance between them and a fortune. The "gradual settlers," the families pushing the frontier steadily west, from the Appalachians and slowly on through "the dark and bloody ground," were still the real pioneers—the best of them neither adventurers nor scoundrels but small, grim people of a puritanical strain who journeyed only to find good soil and achieve nothing more than "their useful toil, their homely joys and destiny obscure."

I think of a family who started a farm on rocky soil in Kentucky: a dim, shiftless, rolling stone of a husband married to an illegitimate girl from the Virginia mountains. He tried five or six farms and kept moving on, a man afflicted, we'd say today, with a character neurosis who thought that by picking a new place, like a movie actress who keeps picking a new husband, he would somehow change the plot. He didn't, of course.

They plodded into Indiana and did a little better. In time, they had a barn and a few animals, a little corral, a rail fence, and they planted corn and flax and beans. But then the neighbors went down with "the milk sickness," picked up from cows that chewed on snakeroot. Our farmer's wife died. So the vagabond father and his dour son moved on to a new state and new ground, the son passing from an almost animal boyhood into a bleak manhood. Yet, out of that frail woman and her listless husband and the poorest ground, there came something strange and wholly admirable: the slow-moving son who seized the Republic and held it through its first cataclysm—Abraham Lincoln.

Overleaf: *In an 1850 photograph, San Francisco Bay is choked with ships, many of them derelict. Passengers and crew alike often went straight to the gold fields.*

6
A FIREBELL IN THE NIGHT

For more than three centuries the Negro in America has been in turn slave, lackey, tenant farmer, hired help, licensed clown and entertainer, who gave to America his cheap labor and his powerful, melancholy music. His lowly status has relentlessly mocked and only very recently challenged the monotonous American declaration that all men are created equal. The Negro has less schooling, worse health, more infant mortality, double or triple the unemployment rate of the whites. He is a permanent invalid in American society. And the places he lives, whether in the town or the country, are its casualty wards.

Let us look over some words that Jefferson put down at the end of a day during which he had seen a planter abusing a slave while the planter's small son stood by:

> The whole commerce between master and slave is a perpetual exercise of the most boisterous passions, the most unremitting despotism on the one part and degrading submissions on the other. Our children see this and learn to imitate it. . . . The parent storms, the child looks on . . . and puts on the same airs in the circle of smaller slaves. . . . And thus nursed, educated and daily exercised in tyranny, cannot but be stamped by it with odious peculiarities. The man must be a prodigy who can retain his manners and morals undepraved by such circumstances.

The blacks of today are not likely to be deeply moved by this passage, except to be soured by the thought that Jefferson went on living out his life at Monticello with his own slaves, who were benevolently treated and attended to his wants without visible rancor or hate. No white man can deride this bitter reaction, for it keeps forcing us to think of what we have suppressed for centuries: the most continuously shameful contradiction of the American heritage.

But it also has to be said that men of all sorts belong always to their own time. Not many whites suffered Jefferson's torments (which must often have been quickened by the memory of a slave killed by his nephew). Few philosophers of the Enlightenment shuddered at the

The sorry truth behind the romance of the antebellum South: a bedraggled family of slaves in a Georgia cotton field, with even the children carrying picking sacks. Reproduced from an old stereograph photo.

189

hanging of a boy for a petty theft. The most humane Greeks in their golden age never doubted that humankind existed in two natural orders, a lower order that labored so that the higher might think fine thoughts and cultivate the arts and sciences.

Today the word "slave" calls up the image of a black man or woman, sold in Africa, by black men, to British or American shippers and put up on an auction block at some port in the West Indies or the American South and then delivered for life to a planter. But the slaves were not always Negroes. In the beginning the laboring whites and blacks under contract were lumped together under one word, "servant," although pretty soon they split up. The vagabond whites, the unskilled, and the shiftless became useless for heavy labor—because they made themselves so—and acquired odd menial jobs away from the fields. The best of the whites became craftsmen, gunsmiths, cabinetmakers, silversmiths, and so on.

And the best of the blacks? It is not possible for us to say what the best of the blacks might have become, for they had no chance to show it. In a warm climate, as Jefferson grimly noted, "no man will labor for himself who can make another labor for him." It never had to be asserted, it was universally assumed, that the Negro was a lower species whom God, in His wonderfully mysterious way, had endowed with a capacity for unremitting heavy labor. That the Negro was considered by civilized men to be exempt from the ordinary decencies can be simply inferred from a very precise drawing of a slave ship submitted to the House of Commons in the early eighteenth century to prove that the seagoing accommodations for slaves were not only ingenious but humane. Here people slept in orderly piles, two or three men on top of each other, an arrangement at once neat and thoughtful, to which, as Charles Dickens wrote in another satirical context, no Christian could possibly object.

Before the slaves arrived they had already forfeited their lives to an as yet unidentified owner. When they were shipped to Catholic Brazil, they could hope to work out their freedom by manumission; they could have no such hope in Protestant North America. They would be set to work on a rice or indigo or tobacco or cotton plantation and watched from dawn to dusk by an overseer. Their whole lives were spent within the confines of the master's domain, and they knew every sort of master, the vile and the chivalrous, the feckless, the good-natured, and the humdrum employers of a labor gang.

The moral or emotional attitude of the owner was not always the determinant of the slaves' treatment. A callow owner might have abundant acres, with a surplus of crops that *somebody* had to eat up. Many plantations were badly managed, not out of malice, but because the owner was always in debt. Even in the golden time of the Cotton

190

Kingdom, there was a good deal of shabby gentility among planters whose own diet and amenities were not much superior to those of their slaves, though enjoyed in larger rooms. On wealthier plantations in Georgia and the Carolinas, the better slave cabins, reserved for the servants of the big houses, might be built of brick. They were one-story, single-room affairs, built by the slaves themselves, with a fireplace and interior annexes contrived by partitions or brick parapets. Here one, two, or possibly three families were born, lived, bred, and died. The laboring slaves had wooden huts in the woods and the fields beyond. The working routine was sixteen hours a day, Sundays off always, and sometimes Saturdays also. Once a week, they were given four pounds of pork apiece and eight quarts—a peck—of corn. They kept their own poultry and grew their vegetables and chopped their fuel in the woods. At Christmastime, and on family anniversaries, they might be given big helpings of coffee and molasses and tobacco, and calico for clothes.

By the time of the American Revolution, half the population of Virginia were black slaves, and in the Carolinas it was two blacks to one white. These figures enlivened, even in the debates of the Constitutional Convention, the old self-protective argument against slavery —namely, all morals aside, the fear of being outnumbered. And by the end of the eighteenth century, there was another historical shift that made some worried planters begin to think again about "the peculiar institution."

The long high noon of the Southern economy was fading into an early twilight. Able young men were decamping to cross the Appalachians. The competition of the West weakened the demand for the crops of the coastal South, and much tobacco land had been worn out by overplanting. Many small planters could make ends meet only by selling off their idle slaves. And the ones that stayed were often a burden on a failing planter: they were susceptible to epidemics (the women, it was often complained, were "poor breeders"). But on one thing most of the Southern coastal planters, if not the Northern shippers, agreed. There were more than enough slaves already on hand. In 1808 the importation of slaves from Africa ceased to be legal.

But it was a ban rarely to be enforced, because in 1794 something had happened that made slaves more desirable than ever. That something was a small invention that produced the Cotton Kingdom. In the autumn of 1792 a young man fresh from Yale College arrived in Savannah, Georgia, and took a boat up the river to the plantation of the widow of General Nathaniel Greene, who had been given it as a reward for gallantry in the Revolutionary War. The young man's name was Eli Whitney. He was the son of a Massachusetts small farmer, on his first Southern journey, going to his first job as a schoolmaster. To a boy accustomed to the winter chores of a snowbound New England farm, his first sight of the South seemed as exotic as a glimpse of Siam; he was impressed and moved by the strangeness of the trees and flowers, the birdsong and the primal life of the bayous. He had struck up an acquaintance with a Southern professor at Yale, and through him he now found himself going to spend a few weeks, before his teaching started, as the house guest of the old soldier's widow.

Whitney was a recluse, an inquisitive brooding type we should call a loner, whose mania was carpentry and mechanics. As a boy he had amazed his family by going off to a carpenter's shop for days on end and reappearing with wheel rims, polished axles, needles, finely ground knives, metalwork, clocks, a fiddle—all of his own construction. He rigged up his own telescope and hygrometer. When a device for measuring the movement of the planets broke down, he talked the college authorities out of shipping it to London and repaired it himself. The president of Yale proudly told his corporation that "the College has been saved Fifteen Pounds by a student who is a remarkable artist."

One evening, sitting at the widow's table and overawed by the Lucullan fare—the muscat grapes and pecans, the rice birds, the little lobsters, the nectarines and peaches, the Madeira and German wines—he listened to some planters reciting a bitter lamentation about the tedium and cost of cleaning their short-staple cotton. It took twenty slaves a whole day to pick and clean twenty pounds of cotton. The problem was an old and nagging one: you had to separate the obstinate seeds from the precious lint before it could be spun, and the one way to do it was by hand. The only machines ever developed simply crushed the seeds and pressed them deeper into the lint. The Southerners talked wistfully about the marvelous spinning machines they used up North, fed by imported long-staple cotton—seventy spindles moved by a single water wheel and run by children. Until the Southerners could figure out how to clean their own Sea Island and green-seed cottons swiftly and cheaply, they could not hope to compete.

Young Whitney had never seen any species of cotton. But he was fascinated by the problem, and in the next few days he settled into a little workshop the family had rigged up for him and tried out various shapes of cylinders, pulling draw-knives over them—but nothing worked. How long it took him by trial and error to arrive at a solution we do not know. But he later recalled, in a letter, the day on the plantation when he had happened to see a cat sitting by the fence that enclosed the poultry yard. It had one paw out through the fence and held it there like a pointer, poised and waiting for a strolling chicken. The paw darted forward and missed the chicken but retrieved a pawful of feathers.

Whitney saw in this a principle of friction and separation, and he applied it to his experiments and came up with a simple box, the cotton gin. Inside it was a suspended wooden cylinder that revolved at the cranking of a handle. The cylinder was encircled with evenly spaced metal spikes that clawed at the deposited raw cotton, shed the seeds behind the cylinder, and let the pure lint come foaming up in front. Whitney calculated that a hand machine like this could do the work of ten slaves, of fifty slaves if it was driven by water. Like so many fundamental discoveries, like the propositions of Euclid, it was so simple that it seemed incredible nobody had thought of it. Once demonstrated, it was indeed so simple that any wheelwright could make it, and it was Whitney's misfortune that most of them did. Trying to monopolize it was like taking out a patent on a shoelace. He did take out a patent, but the accumulating variations obliterated his claim to ownership. Not until he was in middle age was he paid for the use of his gin in the Carolinas and Tennessee. From Georgia, where it was first used, he received next to nothing.

The device gave a gigantic lift to the fortunes of the Southern planters. It caused the arable South to expand into a landscape of cotton, and men who had once kept fifty slaves bargained and bartered for hundreds. At about the same time, another simple experiment turned the hot, wet delta lands of Louisiana into more fortunes and yet another recruiting ground for black slaves. Before, and after, the Revolution all the sugar made in the United States was produced for the household by the householder tapping trees for their sap. Within a year of Eli Whitney's first patent (1794), a bustling little Frenchman, Jean Étienne Boré, invited the people of New Orleans to his plantation outside the town, where he had set up in a shed some crude machinery and some vats. He was apparently something of a Barnum, and he wished to offer a public demonstration that sugar cane could be boiled off into crystals. Toward nightfall, as the vats were cooling off, the first crystals appeared. Boré invited the city fathers to come close and make their inspection, and then he appeared to proclaim, to resounding cheers from the crowd: "It granulates!"

So a sugar empire began to stretch west across the rich lowlands. The next question was how to get the great harvests to the North?

The Mississippi has a powerful downstream flow and whirling currents. Many planters had tried and failed to pull boats upstream with teams of horses plodding along the banks. Then, in 1811, New Orleans built the first high-powered, light-draft steamboat and solved the problem of upstream navigation. They started shipping cargoes of raw sugar

Overleaf: *In an 1861 painting by Adrian Persac, the Olivier plantation in Louisiana breathes calm and prosperity. The plantation's own sugar mill is at right.*

But that, as they say, is *our* problem. The historic fact is that, while the South was spreading cotton and sugar and tobacco and expanding the empire of slavery, the North was committing itself to men and machines and spreading them through the Northwest Territories. Eli Whitney's nagging ingenuity gave a tragic guarantee that the North would welcome the Industrial Revolution and the South would reject it, that the North would go one way and the South another—and that sooner or later they would collide.

As the pioneers flooded into the Western lands, and old territories turned into new states, not only machines followed them but independent farmers who were soundly against slavery. With them it was not simply a matter of principle. They had gone West to work free land for their own prosperity. They did not intend to compete with slave labor. So the awkward question came up: what would happen when the two streams of settlers flowed together *on the same ground*?

"This momentous question," wrote the aging Jefferson, "like a firebell in the night, awakened and filled me with terror. I considered it at once as the knell of the Union." The bell was rung by Missouri's request in 1819 to come into the Union as a slave state. Missouri had been settled by slaveholders, but it lay north of the horizontal line that divided the free states of the North from the slave states of the South. If Missouri were let in as a slave state, a Northerner would look at the map and see a precedent, an invasion, at best a buffer state. In the event, the Congress bowed to Missouri but to maintain its custom of balancing one free state and one slave, it also admitted Maine as a free state. In the same act, it prohibited, from then on, all slavery north of the line of latitude 36° 30'. It is known as the Missouri Compromise line. It was destined to be also a battle line.

This geographical balance lasted, precariously, for about thirty years. But it was thunderingly upset by the United States' war with Mexico, in 1848, out of which the Union acquired vast new lands, most of them south of the Missouri Compromise line: Texas, Territory of New Mexico, California, and Utah well to the north. They had their own strong traditions. Texas had slavery, California had not, and the two territories would test the power to legislate either system. This massive challenge to the compromise greatly aggravated the enmity between the North and South. It quickened the agitation in the North to keep slavery out of all the new states and territories, and it united the Southerners in a kind of self-protective defiance. The new Westerners in the North were

Industry was the North's great strength. At this Cold Springs, N.Y., foundry alone, 3,000 cannon and 1,600,000 projectiles were made for the Union Army.

confirmed in their prejudices, many of them gross and bigoted, about the brutality and peonage of the South. Not all Northerners by any means believed the fire and brimstone propaganda of the Abolitionists, which had been brewing for a quarter of a century. Anti-Abolitionist mobs beat up a Bostonian in 1837. In the same year, in Illinois, a clergyman was killed.

The issue came to a head, as great issues tend to, first in the United States Senate and then in the Supreme Court. The House passed a proviso prohibiting slavery in the territories taken from Mexico and made it apply to Texas, where many slave-owning Southerners had died in the cause of bringing their republic into the Union. The Senate defeated it. What had the Senate to offer on its own account? In the main it had the patriarchal figure of Henry Clay, a bony, awkward Virginian who had gone into Kentucky, become a successful lawyer, turned at twenty-two to politics and given fifty years of his life to a failing campaign to abolish slavery. In 1850 he stood on the Senate floor to make the last speech of his life. He was seventy-three, worn down to the bone and the dewlaps, and he was wracked with arthritis. He talked for two days, and he came up with a solution that fair-minded men, if they had been in a majority, might have accepted with good grace.

On the seething issue among Southerners—the harboring of thousands of fugitive slaves in the North—Clay proposed that they should all be returned to their masters. Let California be admitted as a free state. Let Texas retain the slave system it had always had. And give to the territories of Utah and New Mexico the freedom to decide when, if ever, they should legalize slavery. This compromise was voted and grudgingly accepted by both sides.

Then there set in one of those terrifying, and rationally unaccountable, decades in American life when all the ingenuity, vigor, and hot blood of the country seem to concentrate into opposing channels of fear and self-righteousness. Of course, there were fair-minded men of considerable influence in every part of the country, but they retreated into the quiet desperation of hoping for the best. They were drowned in a boiling sea of rhetoric and provocation. In defiance of federal law, the Abolitionists increased their help to fugitive slaves and got at least fifty thousand of them away by an organized underground. And there was that strange, brave egotist from Connecticut, John Brown, who raided a federal arsenal with the intention of arming Southern slaves. He was caught, tried, and hanged, but his name, if not his soul, goes marching on in a song that was in its day a fearful battle cry. All of this was enough to taunt the Southerners to the point where they talked of secession and meant it. It was left to the Supreme Court, of all healing institutions, to shatter the hope of compromise.

In 1854 and 1855, at the height of the political turmoil over slavery in Kansas and Nebraska, the Missouri painter George Caleb Bingham produced a series of genre scenes dealing with campaigning and voting. This one, dated 1854, was called "The Verdict of the People."

A Negro slave, Dred Scott, from the slave state of Missouri, had lived for some time in the free state of Illinois. He had done so with his master's permission, but when he went home again he sued to have himself declared a free man. The Supreme Court ruled that whether or not it could be argued that a Negro was a citizen, a slave was not. The laws of Missouri were binding. In a word, the Court said that Congress was powerless to exclude slavery from a free state. From that moment on, the two nations—for that is what in fact, and in feeling, they had become—fell almost resolutely apart.

On December 20, 1860, a state convention in South Carolina dissolved "the union now subsisting" between it and the other states. By February 1, the rest of the Deep South followed: Mississippi, Florida, Alabama, Georgia, and Louisiana. Eight days later these six seceding states met in Montgomery, Alabama, formed their own Congress, adopted a constitution, and proclaimed "the Confederate States of America." They were quickly joined by Texas.

In March a new President, Abraham Lincoln, on his own initiative declared secession void and promised to "hold, occupy and possess" all government property. He quickly kept his word. The day after his inauguration he ordered a shipload of troops to land on Fort Pickens, an island fort in Pensacola Bay off the coast of Florida. It was held by forty Union troopers who had escaped there in January, when Southern forces had seized government forts on the mainland. The reinforcements had agreed with the Confederacy to stay on their ship so as not to appear to be raising a dramatic siege. Undoubtedly Fort Pickens would be immortalized in all the schoolbooks if Lincoln's landing order had been obeyed. But there was an unaccountable delay in delivering the order of March 5, and the troops landed, without incident, on April 12, only a few hours after a similar episode far to the north had carried the nation into war.

There was another island fort, Fort Sumter, built on a sandbar in the mouth of Charleston harbor, off the shoreline of South Carolina, the first and most militant of the seceding states. At the end of February the fort's commander warned Washington that he was dangerously short of supplies and in April Lincoln ordered a fleet to go and relieve the Fort Sumter forces. The commander of the Confederate forces invited the garrison to leave. It refused, and at four thirty in the morning of April 12, 1861, the Southerners loosed their fire. In the afternoon of April 13 the Union forces surrendered—and the war was on.

In the slavery debates before the war, various orators and newspapers had picked up a tremulous slogan from the Bible: "A house divided against itself cannot stand." Two years before he became President,

Lincoln had added his own hard gloss: "I believe this government cannot endure permanently half slave and half free. I do not expect the Union to be dissolved; I do not expect the house to fall; but I do expect it will cease to be divided. It will become all one thing, or all the other."

But for two months or more, no such sharp division was made. Virginia first voted against secession and then, five days after Fort Sumter, seceded. Arkansas, Tennessee, most of all Virginia, were neither of one mind nor the other. They all had whole regions where there were no slaves. Eventually Arkansas and Tennessee—its eastern part unwillingly—joined the Confederacy. So did Virginia, but its mountain people were stubborn enough to hold out and form a separate state, West Virginia, which remained loyal to the Union while her people split their allegiance—and their fighting forces—in the ratio of three to one for the Union. North Carolina was the last state to go with the South; and the border slave states—Kentucky, Maryland, Delaware, and Missouri—overcame much hot propaganda to secede and stayed within the Union, hoping against hope to keep cool and neutral.

In many places, among innumerable old Southerners and border state people, the tug of opposing loyalties was never relaxed. "A house divided against itself" had a piercing relevance to the army regulars. They had an immediate duty to decide which side to be on. Two brothers were major generals with the opposing armies. The commander of the Confederate Navy had a son killed in the Union Navy. Mrs. Abraham Lincoln's three brothers died for the South. And we have only to look over the places where the battles were fought and guess the local loyalties of the troops to see that no war is more wounding to the young than a civil war, which turns the homeland into alien country and a map of bloody family feuds.

In the beginning the Northerners thought—as one side always does—that the war would be over "by Christmas." The North had twenty-two million people against the South's nine million. The North had the steel to make its guns and matériel; the South had to buy them from France and Britain. The North had twenty-two thousand miles of unified railroads, and the South had only nine thousand miles of track of various gauges. New York alone produced twice as many manufactured goods as the whole of the South. And so on. Why, then, did it go on for four years?

Few great wars can have swung so sluggishly, so uneasily, between one side and the other. Only in the naval war did one side, the North, establish an early supremacy and hold it. The blockade of the Southern ports froze the sea passage of Southern supplies very early, extended down the East Coast and round into New Orleans, and kept even the South's warships out of their own bases. And in the summer of 1863, the capture of Vicksburg ensured the North's total control of the Mississippi on the Confederacy's western flank.

On land, the record is one of massive and inconclusive thrusts and setbacks. Neither side was at all prepared in any professional military sense, but it has been an American characteristic, from the Revolutionary War to the Second World War, to flout the old professionalism and improvise its own ways of war. The Civil War introduced so many radical tactics—including trench warfare, the night raid, wire entanglements, hand grenades, flame projectors, land mines, armored ships and trains, torpedoes—that it provided the standard manuals for Sandhurst and Saint-Cyr, as well as West Point, even up to the Second World War. (If these academies had learned their lessons better, they would have appreciated by 1914 at the latest the inefficacy of the cavalry charge and the bayonet.) There was only one great engagement in the first year, at Bull Run, and like almost every battle thereafter it was indecisive. For a time, for a long time, the South held the advantage of position, if not of penetration, on the eastern front, while in the West, the Union asserted and usually held the advantage.

There are several battles among which the experts argue in picking out the "typical" engagement. Gettysburg is the popular favorite, as being the last and deepest advance of the South. Shiloh is another, often called "the half-victory," because the Southerners showed their daring in a night raid, because the sagging Northerners were able to call on tough, fresh reserves from across the river, and because the Northerners were then too exhausted to pursue the scattering Southerners.

Personally, I should choose the Battle of Antietam, of September 1862. Not for Lee's brilliant forked invasion of Maryland, with protective maneuvers to the south and west; not for McClellan's countermove to throw three forces at Lee's left, right, and center; not even for the typical Northern blunder of mounting these attacks one at a time instead of simultaneously; nor even for Lee's systematic defeat of all three. But for the all too typical situation in which the Southerners held, the Northerners slumped back in exhaustion to wait for their reserves, and the Southerners then withdrew, having no reserves at all.

Antietam did not set a pattern but it revealed one that foredoomed the South. The South had at the start a huge granary to dip into. For two years it kept the upper hand in cavalry battles, because it could call on a whole society of horsemen. Its generals were at once more adroit and better disciplined, and they developed exceptional skill at fighting along interior lines. But ultimately it came down to the great disparity of resources, of men and matériel, that we mentioned at the start. The South had the audacity, but the North had the reserves.

For all these disparities, camp life on both sides was equally primitive.

Going off to war in their new uniforms, they proudly posed for a daguerreotype portrait. For some, it was the last record. Private Edwin Francis Jennison of Georgia (bottom right) died at the Battle of Malvern Hill in 1862. John Branch (top left) and Robert Patterson (top right), brothers who served in the 12th Tennessee Infantry, survived the end of the war. Who the boy at lower left was, or his fate, remains unknown.

Country boys, until they were talked into a little elementary hygiene, into the magic of carbolic soap, dropped in the plaguey summers like swatted flies. Amputation was the sovereign cure for a badly wounded limb. And if you survived after that, you had one chance in four of dying from infection. But it is one of the maddening facts of war that it can galvanize an embryonic specialty into life. The young science of neurology was forced into startling growth during the Civil War by the unprecedented opportunity to observe the effect of gunshot wounds on the nervous system. Philadelphia, in 1863, set up the first hospital, headed by S. Weir Mitchell, to treat soldiers suffering from "nervous disorders." Various "anti-aesthetic agents" were being rapidly developed in Boston, and the first printed use of the modern word is recorded, under the date 1863, in the Oxford Dictionary of American English: "Dr. Morton attended the principal battlefields, and administered anaesthetics with his own hands." For the last two years of the war, the battlefield use of anaesthetics became routine—among the Northern armies. For while high-minded men and women in the North formed something called the National Sanitary Commission to start veterans' pensions, organize nursing wards at the front, and provide for the human problems of the men going home, for the Southerners there was only the compassion of scattered families, and the hope that the next raid would capture not only food and ammunition but some of the drugs and the chloroform Abraham Lincoln had barred from shipment to the Southern armies.

There was another resource of the South that it may now seem hectoring or sentimental to harp on. This was the Southerners' tenacious conviction, however wrongheaded or unholy, that they were fighting for a principle. Not slavery. Slavery alone could not have united landowners and frontiersmen, merchants and mountain farmers, poor whites (and even black soldiers). The Southerners had a homeland in a sense that the North did not: even today, when the textile cities of the South and the soft-drink factories break up the old agrarian uniformity, the South is still a separate culture—with a literature, an idiom, a diet, mores, a pervading sense of irony, and tragedy—quite alien to the continental American culture in which a Maine potato farmer and an automobile salesman in San Diego are almost equally at home. The Southerners wanted neither land nor conquest. They wanted to prove that their homeland was unconquerable. The names of the places where they tried and ultimately failed to do so still toll through the American memory like an elegy: Vicksburg and Antietam, Bull Run and Chancellorsville, Manassas and Chattanooga and Fredericksburg, Cold Harbor and Shiloh and Gettysburg.

I once met a very old man with a long, chiseled face and a snowy mustache and a blazing eye. He was a New Englander of rather fearsome dignity and reserve. Yet, when he came to put down his entry in *Who's Who in America,* he couldn't help beginning with: "Born March 8th, 1841, Boston. Captain, 20th Massachusetts Volunteers, wounded in the breast at Balls Bluff, in the heel at Fredericksburg, in the neck at Antietam." He survived to become the most distinguished jurist, in his old age, in the English-speaking world. He was Justice Oliver Wendell Holmes. I still find it hard to believe that I once met a man who was wounded in the American Civil War, when I think also that his comrades in arms have been dead for over a hundred years. Their only lasting memorial is the sepia photograph they had taken when they first put on their uniform.

To fuse the unity of the South there was a single commanding hero, another thing the North lacked. He helped the South to fight with a single-minded passion. Robert E. Lee was the son of Washington's cavalry leader, a dashing improvident charmer whose wild speculations left his family bankrupt and himself a dying exile in the West Indies. Young Lee was brought up, by his invalid mother, as the scion of a once "land poor" Virginia family. From about the age of twelve it was his job to "carry the keys," that is to order the food, watch over the dwindling moneys, and more or less bring up his six brothers and sisters. He retained only adoring memories of his vanished father and almost as a filial duty went through West Point. He was put in the engineer corps and saw no fighting till the war with Mexico in 1846, when he was in his fortieth year. He was bright and gentle and professionally known for his ability to match the enemy in surprise but also for a rather regrettable tolerance of his subordinates' contrary ideas. He had one last sortie in the Comanche country and then, like George Washington, he retired. Unlike Washington, he went home to an ailing wife and little money.

When the slavery issue came to a boil, Lee made it quite clear where he stood. He freed his own slaves and wrote: "Slavery is a moral and political evil in any society, a greater evil to the white man than the black." There are some problems of conscience, however, that cannot be so cleanly solved, and when the war started Lee faced an acute moral conflict. It was always a shock to recall that Lincoln offered him the command of the *Northern* forces. He could have taken it on principle because he firmly believed that secession was unconstitutional. But through five generations all his loyalties and his affections were with Virginia.

He spent a day and a night pacing around the bedroom of his house and looking down the slope of the hill that is the last short stretch of Virginia before the Potomac River and the North begins. At the end of this agony, he came downstairs and wrote a letter to his son, in which he said he believed in the Union and could "anticipate no greater calamity"

Seated on pews dragged out of a Virginia church, General U. S. Grant (in front of trees) and his staff officers hold a conference during the Wilderness Campaign of 1864. Lincoln had made him commander-in-chief shortly before.

With horses, troops, and the smoke of cannon fire faintly visible in the distance, this is one of very few actual battlefield photographs taken during the Civil War. It was made by the famous war photographer Alexander Gardner on September 17, 1863, at Antietam, Maryland, probably for the use of magazine artists preparing wood engravings of the scene.

On December 13, 1862, behind this stone wall at the foot of the small hill near Fredericksburg, Virginia, called Marye's Heights, Confederate soldiers stood off repeated assaults by thousands of Union troops. That day the line held. But five months later, at the beginning of the Battle of Chancellorsville, it quickly fell. This picture shows the aftermath.

than its dissolution. "Still, a union that can only be maintained by swords and bayonets . . . has no charm for me [and] if the Union is dissolved . . . I shall return to my native state and, save in defense, will draw my sword no more."

The monumental serenity and gentleness of Lee have provoked many sentimental plays and reams of idolatrous prose. But there might be a fine play in the second moral—and political—conflict he had to resolve: that of never drawing his sword "save in defense" and yet accepting the command of the Southern forces. In any case, he went back to Virginia to fight for a principle that, ironically, Lincoln himself had enunciated better than anyone, thirteen years before Secession. "Any people, anywhere, being inclined and having the power, have the right to rise up and shake off the existing government, and form a new one that suits them better."

The nub of the conflict between North and South was the definition of "any people, anywhere" (how about the people of Virginia?). To Lincoln, it came to mean exclusively "the people" of the United States. The South took him at his earlier word and presumed that any region as closely knit by culture and economics as the South could claim to be a "people" free to assert the right of self-determination. But Lincoln, in his first proclamation of the war, had declared the "combination" of the Southern states to be illegal. And to this day, the historians and popular sentiment have overwhelmingly agreed with him. Yet, it seems to me, we have all been bedazzled by the Gettysburg Address, a small masterpiece of rhetoric of very dubious logic. Its most famous phrase is very close to political nonsense. Quite apart from the anarchy implied in any government *"by the people,"* there remains the ticklish question of how many people or states or ethnic minorities constitute a "people" who may justly wish to govern themselves. Woodrow Wilson held no such bland assumptions about the whole being more sovereign than its parts when he created nations out of ethnic minorities yearning to be free of government by the Austro-Hungarian empire. I'm afraid we must conclude, with Justice Holmes, that the winner is always right.

A few days after Fort Sumter, Lee left his house on the hill and never went back to it. And within a few more days it was a camp and then a graveyard. The Secretary of War, to whom Lee had written a note rejecting the Northern command, saw to it that no one would want to live there again. He ordered that soldiers' graves should be planted close to the house. Later the place was confiscated by the government and became a military cemetery. It is now Arlington, the national military cemetery.

I don't suppose there is a more beautiful, bleak view in all America

Eleven days after he surrendered to Grant, Robert E. Lee stands on the back porch of his house in Richmond. He was reluctant to pose and did so only upon the urging of photographer Matthew Brady, an old friend.

than the one from the porch of Lee's portico, through the fat-bellied Doric columns, looking over the graves of the murdered Kennedy brothers, across the river to the white marble temple that enshrines the memory of yet another murdered President, Abraham Lincoln. He is the man who more than any Northern soldier—more than Grant, the Ohio farm boy—was Lee's moral and political antagonist.

It is difficult, and in some quarters thought to be almost tasteless, to talk sense about Lincoln. But we must try. For the holy image and the living man were very far apart, and keeping them so does no service either to Lincoln or to the art of government. Like all strong characters, he was well hated, and like most frontiersmen who have come to high office—like Harry Truman and Lyndon Johnson—he was ridiculed for his directness and country manners. The London *Times* called him "the Baboon." Lincoln had a gangling gait, a disturbing fondness for rough stories, and a maddening habit of being, in a kind of tooth-sucking way, wiser and sharper than you. (To make it worse, most of the time he was.)

Like all strong Presidents he enraged the Congress by sweeping and arbitrary acts that went, much of the time, beyond the Constitution—or in any case beyond the balance of presidential and Congressional authority that is inevitably tipped in the President's favor in time of war. Indeed, until he was dead Lincoln was never wildly popular. When the war started he used the executive power solely—to proclaim an insurrection, declare a blockade, suspend habeas corpus, expand the army, order emergency spending—and for a year or two he had a dreadful time getting Congress to approve his conduct of the war. Congress would not ratify his acts till the summer of 1861, and it was only two years later that a Supreme Court bolstered with Lincoln appointees upheld him by the whisker of a 5 to 4 majority. Proclamations were his favorite weapon, whereby, most notoriously, he threw thousands of people into jail without trial, on suspicion of treachery or disloyalty. The debunking temptation must nonetheless be resisted. Because he was not a saint, there is no obligation to see him as a tyrant or a hypocrite. He allowed the fiercest freedom of criticism in Congress, in the press, and in public protest meetings. He handed out appointments irrespective of party or military status. He learned very quickly about war, spotted the character flaw in a likable general and fired him, and in the end picked the best. And he was so lacking in egomania that he could tell his generals that "when you are in the field, you are the Union." He had an extraordinary feel for the humanity of quite inhuman people and tolerated them long enough to get them to do what he wanted—contractors, war profiteers, wheeler-dealers, the scum of the Republic. He dignified the trade of politician like few men before or since.

By some brain chemistry that has never been explained, Lincoln

On April 9, 1865, the day of the surrender at Appomattox, Lincoln sat for photographer Alexander Gardner. This extraordinary portrait, which shows plainly the toll of the war years, was the result. Lincoln was never photographed again; five days later he was shot by John Wilkes Booth at Ford's Theatre.

transformed in middle life his whole style of speaking and writing. His early speeches are frontier-lawyer baroque, stuffed with the fustian of his time. We know that he steeped himself in the subtleties of Shakespeare, the cadences of the Bible, and the hard humanity of Robert Burns. And somehow, and conspicuously during the war, he became what he always must have been: a shrewd, honorable frontiersman of very great gifts. Not the least of these was his ability to express a hard, unsentimental truth in the barest language every tinker and tailor could understand:

I have found that when one is embarrassed, usually the shortest way to get through with it is to quit talking or thinking about it, and go at something else.

I have no prejudice against the Southern people. They are just what we would be in their situation. I surely will not blame them for not doing what I should not know how to do myself.

If I could save the Union without freeing any slave, I would do it; and if I could save it by freeing all the slaves, I would do it; and if I could save it by freeing some and leaving others alone, I would also do that.

He exemplified better than any statesman until Churchill the Churchillian line: "The short words are best, and the old words are the best of all."

He is admired, of course, because he led the winning side. He is revered because he wrote—when the South was sure to lose—the Emancipation Proclamation. We often overlook the fact that this stirring document was intended to apply only to the Southern states, and not the slave-owning border states; Palmerston's verdict is still fair comment—that Lincoln undertook "to abolish slavery where he was without power to do so, while protecting it where he had power to destroy it." But the overwhelming aspect of his reputation is that he was assassinated, and so he was canonized, because a halo descends on all the murdered Presidents, and on Lincoln most of all.

At the end of the war, the South was beaten, and—much worse—it was devastated. The Cotton Kingdom was destroyed, the plantation system with all its evils, and its virtues, was debauched. Four million slaves were freed, but with nowhere to go. The land, simply the natural richness of the land and the man-made culture of the South, was defiled. In a single long march of sixty thousand men, from Atlanta three hundred miles to the sea, General Sherman destroyed every town, rail yard, mansion, and crop across a swath of sixty miles. It was a systematic atrocity that haunted Sherman for the rest of his life and made him howl at a graduating class of the Michigan Military Academy fifteen years later: "I am tired and sick of war. Its glory is all moonshine. It is only those who have neither fired a shot nor heard the shrieks and groans of the wounded who cry aloud for blood, more vengeance, more desolation. War is hell."

But the Union was restored. And at what a price! Germany, after the Second World War, was hardly so badly off as the conquered South. It was not only conquered; it was now to be punished. It took the strenuous efforts of General Grant to prevent Lee and other Confederate generals from being brought to trial for treason. The Northern politicians were fearful that if the Southerners were restored to their rights they would form a Democratic majority and leave Congress at the mercy of men lately traitors. So several Southern states were put under military command and many sections were patrolled by Negro federal troops. South Carolina was denied its entire white representation in Congress. Alabama had its governor removed and the government jobs of all ex-Confederates were filled by Negroes; Negroes dominated the state legislature in the proportion of three to one. In other states, Negroes—both able and practically illiterate—made up half the membership of state legislatures.

There were Northern idealists who thought they were seeing in this amalgam the dawn of the equality of man. But throughout the South both the blacks and the whites were puppets manipulated by Northern businessmen and salesmen, who descended on the conquered province like locusts. When the reaction came—and it came swiftly—the Negroes were brutally swept from such power as they had and from all the voting booths—and they didn't enter them again for many decades. The Negro was once again, if he was lucky, a hireling, never to be trusted as an equal. He had been pitied and despised, and on many plantations charitably indulged. Now he was feared. These memories were kept fresh in the South for many generations and planted the trauma from which we are only now painfully beginning to recover.

The Negro might once again be the creature of the Southern white, but, even after the scalawag and the carpetbagger had gone, the whole South—white and black—would remain for another eighty years the poor brother of the Union, the creature of the Northerners in Congress who fixed the tariff and the railroad freight rates. Not until the late 1930s would the South move out of worn land and single crops into valleys and industries fertilized by public power. By that time the South had a population of poor whites listless from malnutrition and other generations of blacks cowed by the doctrine of "white supremacy." And over them both by then stood a raw plutocracy, with the best of the old planter types gone to seed or gone to their shrunken acres.

Overleaf: *The desolate aftermath: scorched and broken, the brick walls of Gallego Mills in Richmond stand in a field of rubble. As capital of the Confederacy, Richmond held out grimly until the very end of the war. But as Grant marched in, and evacuation was going on, the city was swept with fire.*

7
DOMESTICATING A WILDERNESS

Walt Whitman, lying paralyzed in old age on a bed in Camden, New Jersey, spoke for all of us who have been there and back when he recalled his romantic image of the West:

> Those towns . . . like ships on the sea . . . Eagle Tail, Coyote, Cheyenne, Agate, Monotony, Kit Carson—with ever the ant-hill and the buffalo-wallow, ever the herds of cattle and cowboys . . . bright-eyed as hawks, with their swarthy complexions and their broad-brimmed hats, always on horseback, with loose arms raised and swinging as they ride.

The impulse to go back once and for all, to settle in the open spaces or beyond them, is still strong and never stronger than after a war. I doubt that there have been many such disillusioned decades as the one after the Civil War. In the South the idea of representative government had become a tragic farce in the puppet governments of freed slaves and renegade whites set up by an unholy alliance of Northern reformers and calculating money grubbers. In the victorious North a million soldiers returned to scarce jobs and gouging profiteers. For the employed townsman there was a twelve-hour day. The European immigrants started to roll in again, city populations doubled, and the frontier spawned lawlessness. It was too much for some people, and most of all for God-fearing idealistic types, who broke away and in country places founded communes—equality-of-women communes, free-love communes, political and religious communes.

There was a great model already in existence, a community at once religious and intensely practical but also rumored to make a fetish of polygamy, the main cause of its being ceaselessly persecuted. But its followers thought always and only that it had planted the Kingdom of God in the wilderness.

They appeared, in the 1840s, an astonishing body of people, led by a second Moses, that walked into the West a thousand miles beyond the settlers, over the crest of the Rockies, and in a desert basin founded the first successful Western community. They called it the City of the Saints. To the rest of us it is known as Salt Lake City, Utah. But to the Mormons it is Rome and Mecca, the capital of the world.

It was a society conceived in the nightmares of Joseph Smith, a fifteen-year-old boy in a small town in New York State. He was aroused, he said, by a vision in which both God and Jesus Christ appeared and told him categorically that all existing and previous religions were fraudulent. After that, the Angel of the Lord came to him regularly and told him he was the chosen of God to found the one true church. He was to unearth a set of golden plates and translate them, and there he would have his holy guide. The fact is that he translated, at least set down, *something*, which claimed to be a scriptural record of the peoples of the American continent and is known as the Book of Mormon.

Between the vision and the reality stretched seventeen years, and for the faithful they were as frightful as any in the history of American idealism. Smith tried to plant the church first in New York and was persecuted. He and his flock moved on into Ohio and were persecuted again. On into Missouri, where they were beaten, imprisoned, raped, and forced into bankruptcy by the burning of their banks. For the Mormons were not only holier than thou, they were thriftier. Their prosperity was as nauseating as their polygamy, so, always, their banks were burned. They went on into Illinois, where the rumors started that the chosen of God were in fact nothing but wholesale adulterers. Again mobs set fire to their houses and farms, and their banks, and dragged Joseph Smith from jail and shot him. Among his survivors was a quite fearless autocrat named Brigham Young, who decided now to fulfill the prophecy of the dead leader that they would one day build the true temple and the holy city "up in the mountains where the Devil cannot dig us out . . . where we can live . . . as we have a mind to."

Thus, one year after the murder of Smith, Brigham Young and his Apostles, so called, began their tremendous walk on into Nebraska and across the Rockies in Wyoming and into the Great Basin, ultimately to look down on the white flats of the Salt Lake Valley. And Young said, "This is the place." (Some people hold that Smith envisioned a final move to another country. If so, his vision was realized, for when the Mormons arrived in Utah, it was the northernmost province of Mexico.) The "place" was a belt of land reaching three hundred miles down through what is today central Utah. They found it as desert and they made it over into the most fertile stretch of the West, because of the immediate assumption, by Brigham Young and his High Council, of absolute power.

Six days after their arrival, Young put out a set of decrees. Land would be neither bought nor sold; it was assigned to each settler according to his particular skill, and if he failed to make it productive it would be taken away from him. Water and timber resources were to be held in common. The first thing to be done, in the two months left before the fall, was to dig irrigation ditches. Water would be allotted according to the condition of your soil and the needs of your crops, a system that still holds. Next, organized farming expeditions were sent out, each one staffed with a doctor, a carpenter, a miller, a blacksmith—all of them farmers as well. As they spread their crops, they spent days at a time away from the settlement, then weeks away as the winter set in. If their allotted land proved barren they were still not allowed to desert it; they had to try through the growing season to make it fruitful. Obviously some failed, some died in the winter snows, and others existed on thorns and grasses. But against the odds of nature and the interference of government scouts, against cheating whites and warring Indians, they sowed and they reaped. It took half a century to make the desert bloom, but in the end it was done. In the depression of the 1930s the Mormons were the only American farm cooperative that steadily refused all help from the federal government. They stuck to their grim belief that the Lord alone giveth and the Lord taketh away.

In all other civil and criminal matters, the law was the law proclaimed by the High Council of the Church, including a precise code of punishments for such things as vagrancy, theft, disorderliness, and adultery. The last word reminds us of the Mormons' own "peculiar institution," which everybody is impatient to know about, for nothing bothers a man with one wife more than another man with many wives who doesn't even feel guilty. The simple truth is that polygamy was another of Joseph Smith's orders received from on high. He was commanded in a vision to establish a superior order of marriage, and polygamy was it. Once arrived in Utah, the High Council declared it to be a fundamental tenet of Church doctrine. Subsequently, many Mormon leaders shrank from it, but many more practiced it, and the record, curiously, testifies that there was little jealousy, few disturbed children, strong fidelity inside the families, and very harsh penalties for adultery.

Harsher still, however, was the treatment of the Mormons by the federal government so long as they kept up the practice. The railroads finally intruded on their isolation, and once Utah became an American territory the Mormons were forced to mingle and trade with malicious "gentiles" (the Mormon word for non-Mormons) who carried appalling tales to Washington. In time, the federal government refused their territory statehood and overrode the authority of their courts. Congress made polygamy a federal crime and prepared to confiscate all the property of the Church. In the end they had to give in. In the 1890s, fifty years after they had settled, President Cleveland signed an act proclaiming

Utah as the forty-fifth state of the Union. Such polygamy and extramural shenanigans as now exist in Utah are undertaken with the same legal risks as in any other state of the Union.

To this day in Utah, the Church's hold on the social and economic life of the faithful is strong. The Church owns most of the office buildings, theaters, real estate, insurance firms, and banks: a religious monopoly of secular life that is hardly typical of the general run of Americans who domesticated the wilderness. To move at all, the majority always has to be prodded by a fear or inspired by a symbol—and, in the decade after the Civil War, the inspiring symbol was that splendid mechanical beast called "the iron horse."

A century ago, the railroad engine was as magical as a space ship. It stirred the American people with the idea that, once the Civil War was over and the Union was secure, it would be possible to unite the continent in fact as well as in sentiment and political theory—and the railroad train was what would do it. But this was quite an order. The Eastern railroads had extended tentacles only as far as Nebraska, while, at the Western end, existing railroads were running north and south, well to the west of the huge wall of the Sierras. In between was an unbridged gap of seventeen hundred miles or so.

To close this gap was a dream shared equally by businessmen and by romantics. The businessmen goggled over the vision of a continental network of towns and deliveries and customers. The romantics were fetched by the prospect of reliving in comparative comfort the trials, and the spectacular discoveries, of the scouts and hunters, the Mormons and the gold seekers. And by 1865, certainly, there had been a generation or two of footloose and first-rate artists who had touched the imagination of the East with paintings that composed a marvelous continental panorama. They started with the familiar East, but then the curtain went up on the blue Appalachians and, beyond, an ocean of prairie and scudding convoys of buffalo pursued by flotillas of redskins; then the land soared up to the famous Rockies and dipped again to another crumpled plain and semidesert, and then true desert, till the fabulous Sierras unloosed their cascading waterfalls; and over their watershed the continent tumbled in glory to golden valleys and the Lewis and Clark wonder of the sailless Pacific.

Until the war was over the transcontinental railroad was a giant enterprise stalled by much bickering between a reluctant Congress and the Army, which had clamored for it. If it had been left to the government it would have taken another twenty years to complete. But it was a commercial venture, and it was fortunately fed by the adrenaline of competition. There were two railroad companies, the Union Pacific in the East

Still some 150 miles short of the point where they would join with the east-bound Central Pacific line, workmen of the Union Pacific use an ingenious jury rig to lower heavy stones for an abutment over the Green River in western Wyoming.

and the Central Pacific in the West, panting to best each other in slamming down a record mileage of track. And although Congress, once it roused itself to the project, had stipulated that the Central Pacific should stop when it reached the California border (Congress was packed with Easterners), it decided in 1866 that the two companies should build hell for leather and meet wherever they met.

So now began a race that is typically American: in its conception, heroic; in its promotion, flamboyant; in its *dénouement*, comic. Yet, when it was done, it caught the breath of all but the most cynical.

First, the Eastern company sent out location parties, tracing the line and shooing off, or picking off, the Sioux and the buffalo and other busybodies. Then came construction gangs, working in shifts and grading the land by as much—in the flat East—as a hundred miles at a stretch, and behind them the track-laying crews, each consisting of ten thousand men and as many animals. For a single mile of track they needed forty cars to carry four hundred tons of rail and timber, and ties, bridgings, fuel, and food—and it all had to be assembled in a depot on the Missouri River. But the Union Pacific had the twin advantages of comparatively flat land and a continuous supply line back to the East Coast. It was quite different for the Central Pacific, which had to fetch most of its materials, except timber, by sea, twelve thousand miles around the Horn; and that included the locomotives. And whereas the Eastern gangs were recruited from immigrant Irish, from the defeated Southern whites, and blacks, the Western crews came mostly from China. The Union Pacific, it was said, was sustained by whiskey, the Central Pacific by tea.

While the Easterners were racing through the prairie, the Westerners were stripping foothill forests, painfully bridging and tunneling and inching up the mountains. Working summer and winter, it took the Central Pacific two years to hurdle the formidable barrier of the High Sierras. A thousand miles and more back East, the Irish gangers frequently fainted from the midsummer heat, but the company officials were revived by the thought that the government had promised a subsidy of $16,000 *per mile* of track. Once they started to climb the Rockies, it went up to $48,000 per mile, with wide stretches of free land bordering the track thrown in.

With the Westerners over the Sierras, and the Easterners over the Rockies, the two armies slogged along the sage toward each other. The graders actually passed each other along distant parallels in the hope of extra pay for establishing their own line an extra mile or two. When they came in sight of each other, the Irish trusted to their fists, but the Chinese had a preference for pick handles, and after a few cracked skulls the Irish took to gunpowder and fired their charges in the faces of the oncoming coolies. The Chinese reciprocated, but the sport was unprofitable, what with burial costs, compensation claims, and the like, and it was stopped.

On May 10, 1869, the tracks met at a place in Utah they christened Promontory Point. The crews had laid 1,775 miles of track in just over three years. Five days later a special Central Pacific train, loaded with company bigwigs, engineers, and state dignitaries came puffing in from California in a rainstorm. The Union Pacific train bogged down in floods and came shrieking in three days later, complete with its own company directors and official guests, and three companies of infantry and a regimental band. It promised a gallant and decorative ceremony. But in the course of their labor the crews had collected a more colorful assortment of interested parties: saloon keepers, gamblers, whores, money lenders, odd-job rovers. And these, with the cooks and dishwashers from the dormitory trains, made up the welcoming party.

Five states had sent along gold and silver spikes, and they had all to be exhibited and applauded. But the chosen symbol was a golden spike. The great Governor of California himself, Leland Stanford, stood ready to drive it into the last sleeper, a piece of California laurel. The band stopped its tootling. There was a prayer. The telegraph operator, high on a pole, finally connected with San Francisco and New York and was ready to flash the first coast-to-coast commentary. It was a single sentence: "Stand by, we have done praying." Then the Governor of California flexed his biceps, lifted the hammer, gave a mighty swing at the spike—and missed. But the faithful telegraph man had already tapped out the news, and New York fired a hundred-gun salute, Philadelphia rang the Liberty Bell, and a San Francisco paper announced the "annexation of the United States."

The country might take to the railroad as a novelty and a tourist fashion, but the companies saw it as a chain of missing links between the Great Plains and the people who would want, or could be urged, to settle it. Following the success at Promontory Point the railroads were spurred to spread branch lines out south of the central line. And the first community they attracted was not a community at all but the land pirates known as cowboys. The line that started this was one that ended at Abilene, Kansas. Here in the spring of 1867, while the continental line was creeping across the plains, there came a twenty-nine-year-old livestock trader from Chicago named Joseph McCoy. He looked at the railroad and he looked at a map, and he got an idea. He knew there was lush grassland all the way to southern Texas. What would be simpler than to connect a cow with a railhead and make a fortune and, incidentally, add beef to the diet of millions in the East? A methodical man, he decided first to buy the town, which was no more than a few cabins and a saloon on four hundred and fifty acres. Luckily, they were owned by another

At Promontory, Utah,
a flag snaps in a stiff
breeze as workmen,
dignitaries, and
hangers-on celebrate
the completion of the
transcontinental
railroad.

man from Illinois, Tim Hersey, and he sold the lot to McCoy for five dollars an acre. (Mrs. Hersey, a God-fearing pioneer, had one day opened the Bible at the book of Luke and she read there, in chapter 3, verse 1, "The Tetrarch of Abilene in the province of Judea." She liked it, and so she christened a town.)

McCoy now spent the considerable sum of $5,000 getting out advertising circulars and sending riders down to Texas to promise the cowboys a safe trail and a fair price at the railhead. The result was the Chisholm Trail. It started not far from the Gulf of Mexico, in southern Texas, with a breed of rawboned, half-wild cattle with long horns, whose ancestors had come over on Columbus's second voyage. By the end of the Civil War there were about three million of these longhorns, and they roamed no farther than the grass and water they needed. Their normal fate was to be slaughtered for tallow and hides, and on their home ground they could be sold for no more than four dollars a head. But at the end of a thousand-mile trail was Mr. McCoy's bait of forty dollars a head, so feeder lines began converging on San Antonio and then joined to run directly north through largely unsettled country and Indian territory. The trail was blazed by horses and oxen pulling plows, which together cut a wide furrow in the land. The herds moved, two or three thousand at a time, in loose order, with a few picked bulls or steers in the lead—at about a mile an hour. With luck, a herd took three months to arrive at Mr. McCoy's stockyard in central Kansas.

It was never a monotonous journey. Resentful settlers squatting along the trail passed their own laws to forbid the cowboys' passage or, failing that, pestered the herds with planted ticks or alarmed them with fires set in the long grass. Equally resentful Indian guides exacted heavy tolls for crossing their lands, at worst led the herds off into quicksands and vanished. The longhorns were temperamentally as nervous as cats, which was why the cowboys' plaintive lullabies and night herding songs came into being, not as a romantic bit of minstrelsy. The longhorns were apt to stampede at the first crack of a thunderstorm or the first high wail of a coyote. And a serious stampede could mean a per capita loss of ten pounds in weight, or a loss of $10,000 to $20,000 on the herd at the railhead.

A hundred days after McCoy had posted his offer, the village of Abilene heard a thunderstorm of hooves coming up from the south. It was the start of the cowboy legend, and of McCoy's reign as emperor of the cattle kingdom. He had boasted that he could deliver two hundred thousand cattle in his first decade. He was wrong. In the first four years he shipped over two million out of his stockyards. He was one of the rare American promoters whose production exceeded his propaganda. He was, they liked to say, "the real McCoy."

Obviously, a few cabins and some bare acres could not possibly cope with as many as five thousand cowboys paid off in a single night. McCoy did build some shacks and extra cabins. But mostly the cowboys slept out on the prairie and wheeled their chuck wagons into town, parking them in front of their favorite haunts—the saloons, the gambling joints, and the brothels. (The habit spread to other cow towns and coined the phrase "lunch wagon.") At the peak of the cattle trade Abilene was as rough as any town on the continent. Marshals came and went by the simple application of the six-shooter, until the arrival of one James Butler "Wild Bill" Hickok, who was not much like his heroic Gary Cooper impersonation. He was something of a desperado himself, a very sharp dresser and a murderous shot, who could skim a hat into the air and perforate the rim with a circle of bullet holes before it flopped to the ground. Happily, he chose to exercise his marksmanship by joining the law instead of fighting it. And the law in Abilene—and in many more mushrooming cow and mining towns—was a ball-and-cap six-shooter, developed in the Civil War, and very light. Before he came to Abilene Hickok had "registered" forty-three killings, and in the service of law and order he was to notch up a round hundred. He became the most feared mayor Abilene had ever had, and he said it all in one short sentence: "Talk about a rule of iron—we had it."

Through the 1860s and 1870s, the cow towns made the Wild West exactly that. Apart from their attraction for claim jumpers, hoodlums and fugitives from the law, they were the battleground between two natural enemies, the cattlemen and the sheep men. The romantic legend we have so lovingly polished through songs and movies has dolled up the truth of a harsh, sordid, and violent life. The death rate in these cow towns was proportionately ten or twenty times as high as that of New York City in its present turmoil. And out on the range, where never was heard "a discouraging word," but only the bellowing of poisoned cattle, all the feuds and sneaky murders were about three disputed necessities of life: Who owned the cattle, who had the grazing rights, who could secure the water holes?

As bad as the cow towns, and sometimes worse, were the mining settlements, where footloose bachelors hoped for gold or silver but mostly hacked away at copper, tin, or lead. And when they emerged like moles from their dust-choked tunnels, they took a deep breath and raised hell on the streets and in the brothels and saloons before the next descent. Their towns were as impermanent as their livelihood: a vein gave out, and a town would go to dust in a week. The miner, like the

---

Overleaf: *A range hand cuts out a cow and her unbranded calf from an assembled herd. Photograph by Dane Coolidge dates from the 1890s.*

cowboy, didn't domesticate anything. The homemaking—and the first codes of law to protect the homesteaders from the cowboys and their trampling herds—had to wait till the arrival of the first victims of the railroads' campaign to attract not birds of passage but settlers.

The railroad agents rattled around Europe looking for landscapes with failing crops and browbeaten minorities. But, in the early 1870s it was not just the poor and the persecuted who were drawn to the Western plains. There were some bizarre adventurers, none more odd than a party of upper-crust Englishmen who responded to the call of the West as a fashionable caper. One Sir George Grant advertised in the papers for a team of young bloods, perferably remittance men, to join him and found an English colony on a tract of land he had bought from the Union Pacific in western Kansas. Within two years he assembled his team, and they collected their hunting pinks and some horses, and a pack of Southdown sheep and some Aberdeen Angus cattle, and sailed away.

When Sir George got to St. Louis he bought a steamboat and was only slightly put out by the news that in western Kansas there was plenty of wind but no rivers worth the name. Nevertheless, these Englishmen had a fixed and beautiful and very confused picture of the West, which included riverboat gamblers, and buffalo hunts, and fox hunts, and endless nights of poker and faro, and a possible brush with wild Indians and with—who knows?—wild women.

The party dragged its steamboat two hundred miles across the prairie and found a creek. They dammed it up and made a little lake, navigable for eight or nine miles. Then they initiated the new life, which was great fun for a while. There were no foxes and no buffalo, so they shot jack rabbits and coyotes and barged up and down the lake and tended their cattle. This went on for four years. But the infernal summer heat and the withering winters got them down. There was a long drought. And the very few women available were not up to the legendary standard. So in the end the whole thing was, as one of them said, "a deuced bore." Sir George Grant had the satisfaction of seeing the village named Victoria, after Her Gracious Majesty. And he had introduced to the United States the Aberdeen Angus breed of cattle.

By then, only three miles to the north, there were interlopers, a band of Russians who had also answered a Union Pacific advertisement. They were, more correctly, Germans, for their forefathers had migrated to the Volga basin, at the invitation of Catherine the Great, to improve the farming. A century later these so-called Roosians jumped at the offer of a cheap passage and free lands in the dream world beyond the seas. Why should they settle fifteen hundred miles inland, in the empty center of America? Well, like most other immigrant farmers, they had an instinct for the familiar land. They would go where the soil was ready for the very crop that had been their staple, wheat. Each of them brought to America one bushel of their native strain, Turkey Red wheat. They were told that the hard prairie was bad for wheat, but they were a stubborn and superstitious lot and they stayed. Unlike the Englishmen, they could not leave of their own free will. If they failed, they were stuck. The wheat turned out to be a very tough and resistant strain, and it flourished. They called their town after *their* sovereign, Catherine. Twenty years from the time the "Roosians" arrived, Kansas had become the wheat bowl of America, and was to be the granary of the Allied armies in two world wars.

And there were many others, from many countries, who came to arid land and made it bloom. Perhaps they were too readily seduced by the railroads. But all of them were eager to make the most of what was, to any European, an astonishing law: the Homestead Act, passed by Congress in 1862, which decreed that anyone at all could have one hundred and sixty acres of public land free by simply agreeing to work it and produce a going crop within five years. The homesteaders, then, were the first true inhabitants of the plains. They introduced the new and stable element—the family. And they began a raw life with very raw materials. There were no trees on the prairie, so their houses were made of dried sod, whimsically known as "prairie marble," and for fuel they used the dung of the buffalo. Doctors were rare, and there was much sickness and many widowers. And many otherwise healthy women went mad, from the scrimping, the droughts, the burning summers and the polar winters, the loneliness, and the ceaseless wind—which was both the prairie farmer's curse and his blessing.

The windmill was one of the three things that made it possible for a homesteader to make a life. The second was a special plow. The typical iron plow simply could not cut through the heavy matted sod of the prairie, which bakes under a midsummer temperature of 100 degrees and is petrified in winter at 40 degrees below zero. Yet the soil was deep and rich and once it was seeded it was capable of supporting splendid crops. It was left to John Deere, a Vermonter who had moved to Illinois, to invent a plow with a revolving blade and a steel moldboard. It cut the sod and then turned it over.

The third thing, simpler still, was barbed wire. To us it is as dull and obvious as a brick or a sheet of paper, but a hundred years ago it saved the homesteader. He might get a crop and make a livelihood, but where there was no timber he had no way of fencing in his farm. So it was invaded, mostly by cowboys, whose herds stomped in and trampled down the crops. Barbed wire re-drew the domestic geography of a large part of the United States. For the first time it defined the prairie farmer's private property. And it incidentally killed off the cowboy—or, rather, by denying him settled land as open range eventually turned him into a rancher, with his own domain fenced in. The longhorn gave way to quicker-fattening breeds, the Hereford and the Angus. The cowboy rancher too, in time, became a family man, a mechanic, a salesman separating his product from the other man's with the identity of a brand. But at first the cowboys, scandalized by the invention of barbed wire, attacked the homesteaders' fences with wire cutters, and provoked endless battles, legal and bloody, with families whose bales of barbed wire ringed their farms like a protective wall. One whole town of homesteaders in Wyoming was raided by cattle thieves and every living person was wiped out—except a newspaperman, who escaped to tell the tale.

In the end the West was won, with a bleak absence of drama, by the homesteader and his woman, the mother of the first generation raised on the plains. She was mother, mistress, nurse, seamstress, doctor, cook, accountant, comforter, and teacher—and was known and usually treated, even by cowboys and miners, as the untouchable Madonna of the Plains. It was she who first acquired the symbols of respectability, the dignity of a pony and trap, a frame house, and such high-toned city amenities as wallpaper, carpets, pictures on the wall, an organ or a piano. By 1890 it was possible for a strict and pious mother to raise a proud family in a frame house even in Abilene. It was the mother who accompanied the family hymn singing and read books aloud, especially "the good Book," maintaining the frontier tradition, which lasted long—too long, perhaps—in American life; that culture belonged to the women. She made the clothes, and in her spare time the coverlets and counterpanes, and hooked the rugs. You can see the handiwork of such a mother, who went to Abilene in 1892, in a small, high-roofed house on a corner. She wove into a cushion still extant the names of her seven sons. One of them died in infancy, but six of them grew to manhood in this cramped house, and one of them, fifty years later, was able to lay down the law to a boy born in the marble halls of Blenheim Palace: Winston Churchill. The corner house is the boyhood home of General and President Dwight D. Eisenhower.

In the year he was born, the last big tract of Indian land was declared open for settlement, in Oklahoma. The claimants and the speculators mounted their horses and lined up like trotters waiting for a starting gun. The itchy ones jumped the gun and were ever after known as Sooners—as Oklahoma was thereafter called the Sooner State. They raced for the good land and the water holes, banged in their stakes, and hunted around in panic to file a legal claim, for in the previous twenty years much blood had been spilled over disputed land claims. Waiting to oblige them were men in suits and hats standing on boxes labeled "law

With wood rare and expensive, blocks of sod had to do for building on the Great Plains; with no doctors and high mortality rates, it was best to have plenty of children. This family settled in Kansas in the 1880s.

office," to offer early proof that behind every successful American is a good lawyer.

In less than thirty years after the Civil War, all across the "enormous gap" spanned by the railroad, the interior was being conquered and domesticated. The whole sequence had been completed, from bare ground to camp ground to shanty town to prosperous "home town." It was some sort of high-water mark of Western civilization when the Dodge City Amateur Dramatic Society put on *A Midsummer Night's Dream.* The perils of the West had faded so rapidly that soon the city fathers could dress up as cowboys and organize a town band available for weddings and picnics. The Wild West declined into the title of a traveling circus presided over by the veteran slaughterer of the buffalo, Colonel William Cody, now a prosperous impresario and owner of a troop of tame Indians trotted out as actors before large audiences at home and abroad. (They appeared once in the pop-eyed presence of Queen Victoria.)

And the Indians? How about the far-flung tribes that had never heard of Buffalo Bill? Did they just scatter and pine away? Not quite. After the Civil War the government sent commissioners out West to sign a final set of treaties with formerly warlike tribes, to confirm and celebrate their presumed new trust in the white man. They were rounded up in vast internment camps that covered anything from a hundred to a thousand square miles. If these reservations were yet too confining for the nomadic tribes, and if ever they thought of breaking loose, the army was on hand to contain them. Since by that time all the great wandering herds of buffalo had been slaughtered and their skins shipped East, the Indians were obliged to troop to their reservations for a regular ration of government beef. If they stayed away, they would simply starve. From then on they were harmless, if not hungry, wards of the government.

In 1876 the country had a stunning reminder that some of them were not ready to be cowed into a bread line. Out of the blue came the news that one third of the Seventh Cavalry, under the command of General George Armstrong Custer, had been massacred while searching for, and unfortunately finding, a Sioux encampment on the Little Bighorn, in Montana. In its fury and humiliation, the army mapped a series of campaigns to ensure that the Indian would never again be anything but a reservation prisoner. Even the great Sitting Bull, the Sioux leader at Little Bighorn, yielded, was given amnesty, and came home from a safe haven in Canada. (Later he too joined Buffalo Bill's circus.)

Late in the 1880s, however, the subjected Indians were suddenly heartened by news of a savior, an Indian John the Baptist whose heralds came out of the wilderness and went among the tribes offering a miraculous regeneration of their pride and a new and glorious indepen-

By the turn of the century, even the roughest cow towns had been tamed. This farm home in southwestern Kansas boasted all the amenities, from wallpaper to an upright piano.

240

dence. All they had to do was to perform a magical rite—a special Ghost Dance. If this were reverently done, the white man's bullets would be as harmless as hailstones, the white man himself would disappear, and the buffalo would be reborn again and populate the earth. The news of this pathetic ritual was enough to alert, and alarm, the military. Buffalo Bill Cody volunteered to parley, but he had no success—the authorities had sent him to talk with the wrong men. (It is quite possible that the army did not, or could not, know the "right" men. For throughout the white man's dealings with the Indian, there has persisted the balky problem of the Indians' complex and odd—to us—principle of authority. It varied enormously from tribe to tribe, and the Indians themselves were just as often the bloody victims of it. Most tribes have a variety of leaders, not always a hierarchy, and in parleying it is essential to know their separate jurisdictions.)

In any case, it seems certain that the army was spoiling for a show-down. A great many of the regulars, having survived the Civil War and seeing their careers coming to a humdrum end when the Indian wars were finished, went off to practice a random "extermination policy" of their own. The fourteen-year interval between the Battle of the Little Bighorn and the final massacre at Wounded Knee, South Dakota, is dark with mischievous examples of bodies of the military taking off on small expeditions to bait handfuls of Indians into hostility, to slaughter them, and earn a medal.

In the autumn of 1890, near the reservation town of Pine Ridge, South Dakota, the Seventh Cavalry, the same regiment chopped up at the Little Bighorn, mustered for the kill. This time they brought up cannon—they were taking no chances. Their jumpiness was aggravated by the news—false, as it turned out—that Sitting Bull had been shot, and the Seventh rode to seek out a band of suspected Sioux renegades. What they found were two hundred men, women, and children. Without a parley or any attempt to establish that this horde was a band of warriors, the Seventh annihilated them, and the next day dug the bodies from the snow and buried them in a common grave. This wretched episode was known to the white man, and still is, as the "battle" of Wounded Knee.

That was the end of it. Throughout three centuries, there had been, here and there, good, even magnanimous, relations with the Indians. But the ruthless continental fact is that wherever the Indians had something that the white man wanted, the Indians lost it—by expulsion, by warfare, by a raft of treaties signed and treaties broken. What the white man wanted, ultimately, was North America, and he took it. In J. Russell Smith's tart epitaph: "The white man banished the Indian to lands where no white man could possibly survive. The Indian fooled him. He survived." And so, after a fashion, he still does.

Today, in many a Western town, on the anniversary of its founding, a skittish annual ritual is performed. The men prance on rearing steeds to the music of a band. The women ride in covered wagons; and the Indians, wherever they are available, consent to get themselves up in the old battle finery and jog along to demonstrate their status as picturesque dependents. The yearning for the open spaces and the free buccaneering life still nags at the American male, as it haunted Huckleberry Finn and kept him in flight from the tendency of women to lasso a man and tie him down. "She was goin' to civilize me," moaned Huck, "[but] I had been there before." We have all been there before. So today the Westerner likes to do for show or sport what his grandfather did for survival. Yet, like you and me, he rides mainly on the Interstate. His hitching post is a gas station with a gift of green stamps. He is corraled in towns and wind-blown suburbs and, even in the old wilderness, is tethered by a mortgage, a parent-teachers meeting, by galoshes, car insurance, alimony payments, and the other ties of domestic bliss.

Overleaf: *Wearing a top hat and sitting at the wheel of a Locomobile touring car in 1905, the 76-year-old Apache chief Geronimo was a pathetic caricature of the warrior who had terrorized Arizona a quarter of a century before.*

8

MONEY
ON THE
LAND

In the early 1820s, only four or five years after Illinois had graduated from a territory into a state, an Englishman crossed the northern section and remarked on an obvious fact that never fails to strike the West Europeans: "The eye sometimes surveys the green prairie without discovering on the illimitable plain a tree or a bush, or any other object, save the wilderness of flowers and grass."

It was something that also struck, and intimidated, the first white settlers, who had moved out of woodland and hill country onto a flat plain with no woods and, therefore, with none of the familiar materials for the making of houses, fires, and fences. So in the beginning the *prairie* was left to the Frenchmen—to the trappers and the hunters —who had christened it. The Anglo-Saxons, and the early immigrants from northern Europe, built their houses along the river bottoms where there was sometimes timber. One of the first handbooks for intending immigrants laid down the necessities of life as "a pair of good horses, a wagon, a cow, a couple of pigs, several domestic fowl, two ploughs (one for breaking the prairie, and the other for tillage) together with a few other tools and implements. . . . A log house can soon be erected."

This prescription anticipated the farmer's usual life on unusually tough soil without suggesting, however, the special richness of a sort of land that has no trees. The prairie was looked on not as an asset but as an impediment, yet one that a patient and resourceful family might overcome. Such a family could learn, it could try at least, to exterminate the pestiferous prairie dog, or gopher, and then snatch a new food from the grouse known as a prairie hen, and even discover a useful medicine in "prairie bitters," a beverage made from a pint of water and a quarter of a gill of "buffalo-gall."

Yet even while these early settlers were battling the prairie as a large natural enemy, there were men alive who began to see what machines might do to reap its vast resources. And at the same time, there were other men who saw the possibilities of reaping fortunes not from the

Some of the greatest fortunes of the nineteenth century started in bleak storefronts like this one in the northwest Pennsylvania oilfields. Impressive name and all, however, the Central Petroleum Company has vanished.

crops that lay *on* the land but from the resources that lay *under* it.

If we retrace the steps by which America went from a wilderness to a giant of technology, there are less than fifty years from the homesteader growing his food on the quarter section (one hundred and sixty acres) that the government had given him, to mammoth factories processing and packaging food for this nation and other nations. Less than half a century from a village on the prairie to the "first city of the plains" —Chicago, the city that more than any other in the world has had its greatness mocked by the curse of a violent legend. To most of the world, it has been in turn the scene of a devastating fire, a stage set to accommodate the gang wars of Al Capone, and the natural setting for the ugly riots that defamed the Democratic Convention of 1968.

It is about eight hundred miles inland from the Atlantic and for countless centuries was known only to the Indians. Then it was a trading post for French fur trappers. It lies on the southwestern corner of Lake Michigan, which is something less than half the size of England. This was the first of four lakes—Michigan, Huron, Erie, and Ontario—that were linked with canals to the north and east, giving clear access all the way from the Atlantic, fifteen hundred miles away, to the western shore of Lake Michigan. At that point, at Chicago, there was a snag—literally, an obstacle that impeded navigation. Between a bend in the Chicago River and the lake there was a sand bar. Once they cut through it, Chicago had a harbor. This was done in 1833, when the place was a squatter settlement of two hundred souls.

When the canal opened, the usual horde swept in: disappointed factory workers from the East, refugee farmers from the rocky soil of New England, immigrants from Europe. Two years later, when the traffic of the Lakes was beginning to hum, a thirty-year-old hustler from New York State arrived. William Ogden was an orphan, but of comfortable means, who had got out of school as soon as he could and at fifteen was already dabbling in real estate. He fancied, he once said, "I could do anything I turned my hand to, and that nothing was impossible." He entered the New York State Legislature on an election promise to build the New York and Erie railroad. But a land company excited him with tales of the boom-to-be along the shore of Lake Michigan, and in 1835 he went to look over a patch of Chicago land his brother-in-law had bought. He was as exhilarated, at a distance, as the Northerners who were sold a slice of paradise in the Florida land boom of the 1920s. They found their plots were underwater and sometimes under the sea. He found a piece of unbroken marsh, and he was disgusted. But he roamed around the rude village and imagined a metropolis. It would have been absurd, had he not made it come true.

Within a couple of years Ogden had been elected mayor of a town of four thousand. He poured money, lots of it his own, into literally hundreds of bridges, sewage plants, water systems, parks, and hundreds of miles of streets that went nowhere. And having created the shell of a city, he now began to fill it. There weren't many carpenters, and there wasn't much time, either, for planing beams and fastening them with pegs. Ogden heard about a new sort of house, a"balloon frame"—a light frame of two-by-fours nailed together so that the strain goes against the grain—and he plumped it in thousands on the land. Today, three houses in four in America are built in this way.

Ogden gambled on the furious growth of the city and in 1841, six years after he'd arrived, the first bumper crop on the prairie paid him off. Wagons brought the crops and the livestock into Chicago; and steamboats, brigs, and schooners carried them to New York and then to Europe. In only nine years Chicago had gone from a marshy village of two hundred squatters to the largest grain market in the world. It became the reception center for all the harvests and the livestock of the prairie. It is still the stock exchange of the American farmer. Every Wednesday, on the floor of the Chicago Commodity Exchange, there is a deafening frenzy of bidding that will be filtered, at twilight, over thousands of radio stations, into a few laconic phrases: "Wheat up one point, corn down three eighths, soybeans steady."

After the Civil War, more ships cruised into Chicago than into the six busiest ports of America combined. But the lake and the river traffic alone would not have made Chicago the mammoth among inland cities. It was the coming of the freight train that did it. Chicago became the ideal junction between the harvests of the encircling prairie and the people, thousands of miles in all directions, who would eat and use them. Because Chicago was where it was when it was—bang in the middle of the prairie—it became the biggest railroad center in the world. It has been host to more than half the presidential nominating conventions. Nowhere have more animals and raw crops been so dramatically transformed. A cow went into Chicago as a cow and went out as a steak or a tennis racket.

The scope of this immense transport system, and the novel ease of it, spurred the prairie to produce far more than the ordinary homesteaders could possibly grow. The raw materials—the soil and the seed, the sun and the rain—were there over millions of acres, but not all the small farmers in the world could satisfy the giant maw of Chicago. Their livelihood, it now developed, was based on a false assumption about the basic American farm. The Founding Fathers, remember, had never left

---

Overleaf: *Between 1860 and 1900 more than 400 million new acres came under cultivation, in part because of such machines as Cyrus McCormick's reaper.*

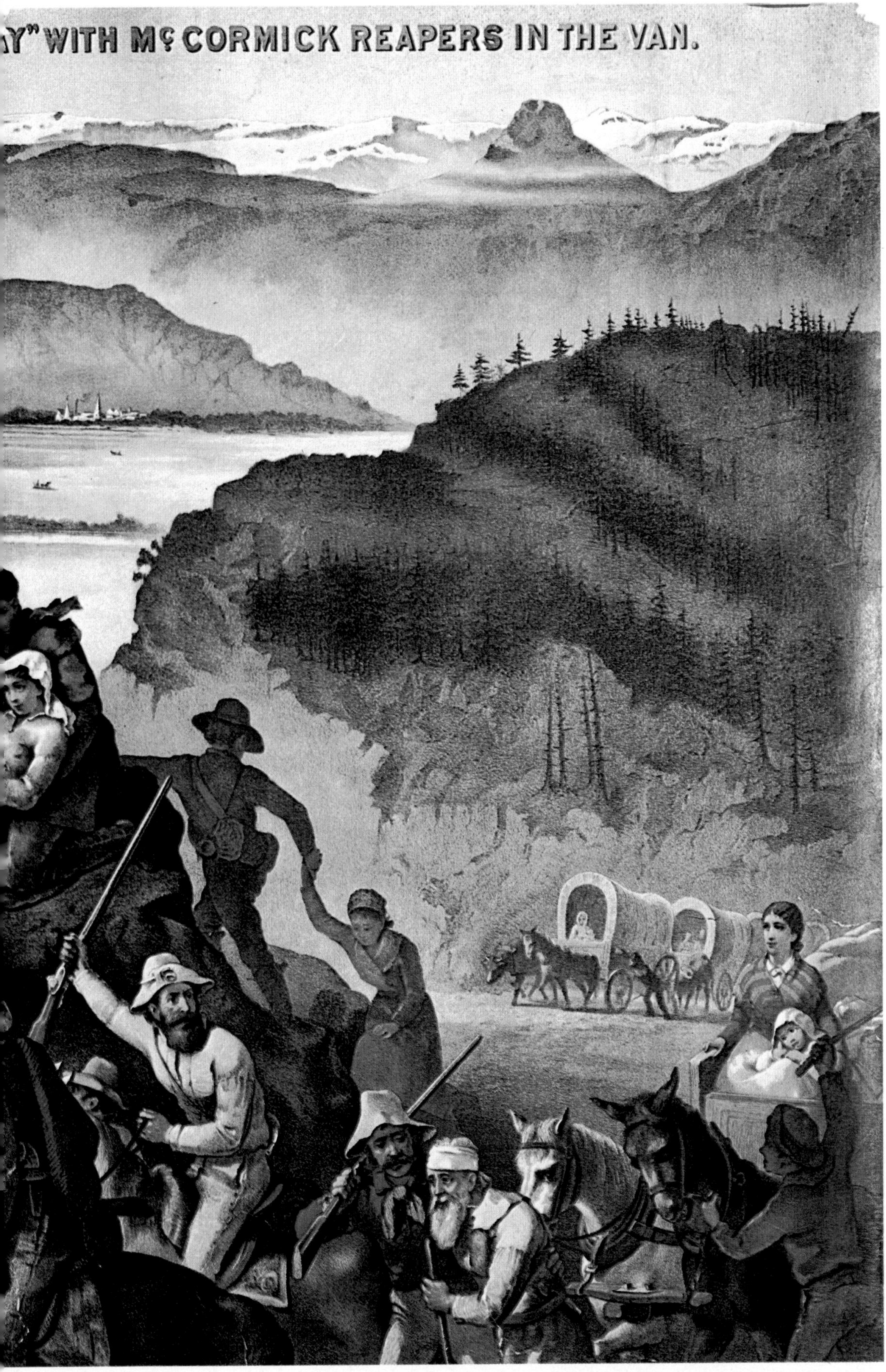
AY" WITH Mc CORMICK REAPERS IN THE VAN.

the East. Their idea of an expanding American agriculture was Virginia or Massachusetts going on forever: parcels of land happily alternating pasture with woods and little rivers, farms that were self-sufficient and suited to a single family.

But the prairie was not like that. One man's quarter-section, of one hundred and sixty acres, the standard square homestead struck off in the thousands on landmaps back East, might have the luck of good soil, a creek, and a few shade trees. But another man's *sixteen* hundred acres might be as hard as cement and barren of all shade and water. Many, many families who went into the Midwest with high hopes of self-sufficiency got badly bruised. Their acreage was too arid or too tough to work, the weather—droughts, hailstorms, winters—had a savagery beyond anything they had known, or a railroad land agent armed with a dispossess notice came by to buy them out for a song. The disenchanted had a bitter rhyme: "In God we trusted, in Kansas we busted."

What Ogden foresaw, and Chicago confirmed, was that, if farming was going to prosper far into the heart of the continent, it would have to turn into an industry. The machines appeared, setting the now characteristic American rhythm of the new need and the new invention to meet it. Ogden invited to Chicago a young Virginian, Cyrus McCormick, to mass-produce the mechanical reaper he had been demonstrating in the East. Before McCormick they cut wheat by hand with a scythe and cradle. His machine did the work of five men, with obviously less fatigue. And so, suddenly, Pennsylvania and Ohio were no longer the big wheat states. The breadbasket moved a thousand miles west—and it was a lucky thing, because the population of the United States went in forty years from thirteen million to sixty million, and Mr. McCormick's mechanical reaper guaranteed that they would be fed. After the reaper, there came in tumbling succession the automatic wire-binder, and the twin binder, the threshing machine, the combine, mechanical corn planters and corn cutters, huskers, shellers, the cream separator, the potato planter, the hay drier. America discovered many decades before Europe that land can be seen as a gorgeous deposit of raw material ready for mass cultivation and shipping and processing and packaging.

This realized ideal of "the farm industry" was a far cry from the original American ideal of the sturdy independent small farmer who made all his own farming and building implements, made the tallow for the candles and the soap, raised a few crops and a few cattle, and tapped the trees for the family sugar. Yet, by a familiar human contradiction, the faster this ideal faded, the more it was mooned over. Millions of Americans bought prints of old farming scenes in the hope of asserting as a sacred fact of American life what was already becoming a memory: the idea of America as a continent without cities, a far-flung republic of yeoman farmers.

But it was not only the conversion of farming into an industry that produced new cities across the country, cities that received, processed, and shipped the crops that lay above the ground. The resources of America are as far-flung as its geography, and, in Western landscapes that had seen more snakes and gophers than pigs and wheat, other fortunes were suddenly discovered to lie under the ground, and in the 1860s and 1870s, throughout the Rockies and the Sierras, those fortunes were unearthed. In 1858 traces of gold were found in Colorado and one year later there was a city that had, first, a hotel and a jewelry store and then the crowning symbol of the miner's prosperity—the "Opry House." Lumber sold in Denver for $100 per thousand feet; and sugar, coffee, and tobacco for their weight in the only going currency—gold dust. In Nevada, in 1859, scratching gold miners cursed the "black stuff" that made the recovery of gold difficult—until they had the stuff assayed and discovered that it was silver of unbelievable richness. A camp site of miners living like tenting Indians could turn in three years into a city of thirty-five thousand with five newspapers and gas lighting on the streets.

By the 1870s, with the war long over and the railroads stretching wider, America began to spawn small cities like rabbits. They grew wherever the railroad loaded produce or unloaded food and necessities. They were places of humble comfort, whose inhabitants wore cowhide boots and sat on Windsor chairs on bare floors and filled the evenings with the wail of the harmonica and the jew's-harp. But as they prospered they started asking for things that it would have been foolish to dream about in their parents' time. Heat and light, news and conveniences, and more sophisticated kinds of entertainment—something better than the local dramatic society and (as Will Rogers liked to recall) the Saturday night excursion downtown "to watch haircuts." It's hard to say whether the prairie communities yearned for city amenities, or whether the amenities were thrust upon them. At any rate, the era inspired a rush of inventors and the heyday of the Ingenious American.

When Samuel Morse flicked the switch that passed out the first telegraph message, somebody said that Maine could now talk to Florida. In Boston Ralph Waldo Emerson remarked, "Yes, but has Maine anything to *say* to Florida?" It is a good question, and one worth asking again in an America that floods the television screen with words and pictures from dawn to dawn, mainly because the television screen is there. But, in the last quarter of the nineteenth century, New York and Chicago had lots to say to each other, and to Denver and San Francisco, and the whistle-stops in between. And just as the railroad and the McCormick reaper combined to spark a mass production system for the farmer, so there was one man more than another who was inspired to mass-produce conveniences for remote towns that either improvised them or had never heard of them.

This man was Thomas Alva Edison, born in 1847 in a small town in Ohio and brought up in Michigan. The extent of his education was three months in a public elementary school. At twelve he was a railroad newsboy, and at fifteen a telegraph operator in various cities. Like Eli Whitney, he had been born with an itch to take things apart and see how they ticked; Edison then tended to put them together again and make them tick louder and longer, at half the price. At nineteen he took out his first patent, for an electrical vote recorder. A year or two later, he was working on a telephone. And, knowing well enough what New York in a hurry would want to say to San Francisco, he invented the stock ticker.

By the 1870s Edison had laid out, and crammed with scientific gear and instruments, not exactly a workshop but in rudimentary form something that not even the universities had—the first scientific research laboratory. He was neither a tinkerer nor a pure scientist who disdains practical utility. His genius was of a quite different order. He put to himself the right question at the right time: how to make a scientific principle workable as a universal convenience. If Edison had discovered gravity, he would have wondered how gravity could help the farmer and the grocer. He could admire the delicate workmanship of a Swiss watch, but wonder, How do you make a dollar watch?

His extraordinary tenacity when he thought he was on to something was most dramatically illustrated by his famous ordeal with the incandescent lamp. In the 1870s the most advanced common form of lighting was gas. The arc light had been developed in various expensive and clumsy forms, but what Edison wanted was a cheap filament in a small bulb to provide an electric light for the ordinary householder. To most of his contemporaries, to the gas companies most of all, this was about as sensible as ordering up a cheap family-sized space ship.

Edison mobilized his small staff with the sense of mission of an explorer headed for the Arctic wastes. He expected from the team the same dedication—and routine insomnia—he imposed on himself. He tried all sorts of conductors—metals like irridium, chromium, platinum. They overheated, they required enormous current, they oxidized. Edison now started a trial of endless materials, plausible and preposterous. Fibers, papers, hemp, bark, cork, and lemon peel. One day he plucked a hair from a friend's beard. But everything kept failing. He needed a tiny, tough, high-resistance filament that would burn in a vacuum.

In the end, he picked up a shred of sewing cotton. He carbonized it, mounted it on the electrodes, pumped out the air to one millionth of an atmosphere and then started to feed the power through Bunsen batteries arranged in series, increasing the current as he went. It didn't overheat. It

With three friends, Thomas Edison (left) perched on an old mill wheel during an outing. The others were also men of note: John Burroughs, the famous naturalist; auto maker Henry Ford; and Harvey Firestone, whose rubber company was the largest in the world.

stayed cool and alive for forty-five hours, and he knew that a solution was in sight. Next day he found that cardboard worked, but not well enough to suit him. He then conducted a test of six thousand vegetable fibers, and eventually he found a Japanese bamboo that lasted a thousand hours. And for the first time the world was lit with electricity.

Edison's creation of the "permanent" electric light swept the headlines, but some of its early users were scared by it. Mrs. Vanderbilt, the Fifth Avenue hostess, went into hysteria when two crossed lines started a fire. City governments were slow to take any risks with this hazardous gadget, though factories, and even ranches, started to install Edison's "lighting plant." And so did theaters. An attractive thing about Edison was that, until he was convinced of success beyond all reasonable, or unreasonable, doubt, he assumed total responsibility for his inventions. He was present at the first theatrical performance to be lit by electricity, a production of *Iolanthe.* After the intermission the lights began to waver and dim and go red. Edison dashed down to the cellar, stripped off his dress clothes, and started shoveling coal in to maintain the steam pressure. He went on shoveling throughout the banquet that was being given upstairs in his honor.

He rarely paused to wallow in the oceans of flattery that surrounded him. He always had thirty or forty ideas in his head, and before he died, at eighty-four, he had blitzkrieged the government with over a thousand patents. He would come into his lab in the morning, pat his pockets, sort through a wad of little notes, and toss one to an assistant. One day he left a scrap of paper on the bench of a man named Kruesi. It contained a drawing so primitive that it looked like a comic-strip joke. In the bottom corner was the note: "Kruesi, make this. Edison."

"What," asked the puzzled Kruesi, "will it do?"

"It will talk back," he replied.

It did. Edison had come on the simple, revolutionary discovery that a steady needle engraving in depth on a revolving cylinder of tinfoil can record the reverberations of the human voice—and that they can then be played back and amplified by the same horn that had received the original sounds. It was the start of the phonograph.

In the thirty-five years between the end of the Civil War and the end of the century, the golden time of American inventiveness, the United States Patent Office granted more than half a million patents. Alexander Graham Bell produced the miracle of the telephone; George Eastman, the handy family camera, a marvel known in all languages as simply a Kodak. And there was the home sewing machine, and the typewriter

Accompanied by the usual phalanx of lawyers (and several delighted messenger boys), John D. Rockefeller leaves a New York court after testifying in an antitrust suit.

(invented, oddly, fifty years before it caught on), and an immense improvement in dynamos and motors. And, capping this great age—which declined as the loner in the woodshed gave way to teams of technologists in labs—was the achievement of Orville and Wilbur Wright with the heavier-than-air flying machine.

At the very start of this machine age there was something else, not an invention but a discovery, which helped transform this country from a farming republic into an industrial colossus. It began by a river in the Alleghenies, in western Pennsylvania. For a century or more Pennsylvania farmers had found their streams muddied by a kind of black glue. It turned up with good soil. First, the farmers cursed it, and then, on an old tip from the Indians, they bottled it and sold it as medicine. As early as 1849, the owner of a salt well put out the "black glue" in pocket-sized bottles with his own printed label: "Genuine petroleum. None genuine without the signature of Samuel Kier." Kier's petroleum was touted far and wide as a cure for asthma, rheumatism, gout, tuberculosis, cancer, and fallen arches. (We do know that, as early as the Revolutionary War, it was a sure remedy for constipation.) A man then discovered that it made a pretty good, though smelly, lighting fluid. After that came a distillation process that produced a purer liquid, almost odorless when burned —kerosene. And in 1859 came the bonanza.

The owner of a tract of land that ran along Oil Creek decided that somewhere underground there must be a primary source for the scum from the creek that Mr. Kier had bottled so profitably. The landowner hired a middle-aged railroad conductor, one Edwin L. Drake, locally given the honorific of "Colonel," who was similarly inquisitive and had tried tapping wells by pick and shovel. He found an ooze of oil, but, after his men had nearly drowned when an underground spring erupted into the shaft, Drake concluded that oil lies deeper than water. He got a blacksmith, who was used to digging salt wells, to sink a seventy-foot shaft by a steam-drill process, and on a sweltering afternoon in August 1859 the black glue bubbled into a flood. The blacksmith jumped on his mule and jogged into Titusville crying: "Struck oil! Struck oil!" He had indeed hit on the first petroleum well. Everybody and his cousin descended on Titusville with mules and shovels and drills and moving platforms, and oil towns sprouted like weeds. Within thirty years, in a sprawling mass of shanty towns along Oil Creek, they were producing thirty-one million barrels in a single year.

There was no central system. It was Everyman for himself, in the well-established American tradition: discover a new resource—a turpentine forest, a seam of coal, a vein of silver, a gusher of oil—work it to exhaustion, ravage the land, and move on. And most of these first oil towns produced their fill and then went back to the grass and the wind.

What the oil business needed was organization.

The organizer was a prim, methodical twenty-one-year-old from Cleveland, Ohio, a smart bookkeeper who had saved his pennies and become a junior partner in a produce commission firm. The year after Colonel Drake's strike, a group of money men in Cleveland sent John Davison Rockefeller off to Oil Creek to look the situation over and report on the long-range possibilities of the gushers. He was not well received by the wildcats, one of whom called him "that bloodless Baptist bookkeeper." Another was to say later that he not only had foresight but "could see around the corner." After his first survey he went home and blandly reported to Cleveland that oil had no commercial future. It is clear that he didn't believe this; his report was more likely an early sign of his gift of protesting a lack of evidence while holding back "something for the lawyers."

He had sensed or been told that the black glue was not necessarily an end in itself. It was still oil for lighting, but Rockefeller guessed it might become oil for heating, for steamships, for lubrication, for power. He had heard the new word "refinery," a word that appealed to a neat young city man, as the crude wells and their cruder owners had not. He and his partner heard of a candlemaker who had refined lard oil and was moving on to petroleum. His responsibility to the Cleveland money men at an end, Rockefeller and his partner pooled their savings and invested all of $4,000 in the candlemaker's refinery. Very soon, Rockefeller got richer men to build more refineries, and richer men still. Since his habits were more austere than theirs, he absorbed them. And then he sat back and he dreamed a dream. He was of the type of Columbus, and Fray Marcos, but with a gift for double-entry bookkeeping. There really wasn't anything to stop him making his refinery business in Cleveland the biggest in Ohio, the biggest in the Midwest, in America. Why not the world? When he was thirty, he formed the Standard Oil Company of Ohio and bought twenty-five refineries.

Rockefeller built a monopoly by means both genteel and ruthless, and it was rudely hinted that he had in the palm of his hands the best state legislatures and United States Senators that money could buy. He not only got the railroads to give him secret low rates because of the colossal business he could throw their way; they secretly guaranteed him a bonus from the regular rates that all the small producers had to pay. When the arrangement leaked, it provoked a national outcry. But Rockefeller rode out the railroad scandal by the well-known expedient of sitting back and letting himself become a beneficiary of the lapse of time. He was only

---

Overleaf: *Thomas Anschutz painted this scene outside a steelworks in the 1880s. It was his only famous painting and it sold for a record-breaking $250,000 at auction in 1972.*

Thos. Anshutz.

is a stinking fish"; "the man who dies rich dies thus disgraced." He started to disembarrass himself of his huge fortune, we should not forget, before the government would have saved him the embarrassment by taking it anyway. And, by an irony that galled him, he began with a church organ. A Scottish Presbyterian church had written and asked him for a pipe organ. It seemed a small thing, and before much could be made of it he provided it. But the gift was hailed first in the Scottish newspapers, and then in the American and the overseas press. In the next forty-odd years he found himself donating, around the world, over seven thousand pipe organs. And because, as a boy, he had had the first apprentice's card to a free public library in Pennsylvania, he gratefully presented over three thousand public libraries in America, Britain, Europe, Africa, and Fiji.

Of his attested $400,000,000, $350,000,000 went to public benefactions, another $20,000,000 to an endowment for peace, and the remaining $30,000,000 to support his old tenants, crofters and servants, and innumerable old friends (including $10,000 a year to David Lloyd George). He pensioned off the widows of former Presidents of the United States. (Congress blushingly caught up with him a little later.)

"The man who dies rich dies thus disgraced." By his lights, Carnegie was not disgraced. He left to his widow and daughter a trust fund that would keep them in considerable comfort, but only through their lifetime, for he maintained that the most evil possible use of money was to leave it to your own family. "I would as soon," he wrote, "leave my son a curse as the Almighty Dollar." Never having had a son, he was saved from risking this malediction.

As he sat in his castle and looked out over the splendid hills and the still lochs, he liked to think of himself as a simple Scottish laird who had given to America more than he took. It wasn't, however, a bad place to be when his steel workers—determined to organize in a union—were shooting it out with an army of strikebreakers hired by Frick. Carnegie was stung by the suggestion of a United States Senator from Indiana that he was "skulking in his castle," and, when the British press took him up on the killing and wounding at his Homestead plant, Carnegie made the mistake of publicly wallowing in self-pity. He swore he had received a telegram from his workers beginning "Kind master," and seeking to know only his wishes. The telegram was never found in his papers. The press of two continents rounded on him as a sanctimonious fraud. The St. Louis *Post-Dispatch* wrote:

Count no man happy until he is dead. Three months ago Andrew Carnegie was a man to be envied. Today he is an object of mingled pity and contempt. . . . [He ran] off to Scotland out of harm's way to await the issue of the battle he was too pusillanimous to share. . . . Say what you will of Frick, he is a brave man. Say what you will of Carnegie, he is a coward. And gods and men hate cowards.

The Glasgow Trades (Union) Council formally proclaimed him "the new Judas Iscariot." He was never quite the same again, and his stifled guilt undoubtedly built up some of the pressure that burst, nine years later, in a shower of philanthropy.

But his feeling against inherited wealth was genuine enough. The people he truly despised were the pack of self-aggrandizers, the sons and daughters of the new fortunes in coke and tin and copper and iron and streetcars and railroads who wanted only to flaunt their wealth in some private Versailles. They found it on the rocky coast of New England, at Newport, Rhode Island. Newport had once been a haven for religious dissenters out of Massachusetts and later a capital port of the slave trade. One hundred years after the Declaration that "all men are created equal," there began to gather in Newport a colony of the rich, determined to show that some Americans were conspicuously more equal than others. They became, in a manner of speaking, dukes and princes by buying or reproducing the trappings of the old dukes and princes of France and Italy. To display these trophies, they built summer houses of the appropriate style and scale. And if you needed a bloodline, Tiffany's of New York would improvise a suitable coat-of-arms. These first- or second-generation rich built what they always called, by a typical affectation of the day, "summer cottages," a name that would have been suitable only if they had been flanked by Blenheim or the Taj Mahal.

The "cottage" of the Vanderbilts, a massive Renaissance palace, was built by the mentor of the Newport colony, the third generation of a fortune originally assembled by the captain of a ferry boat that plied between New York and New Brunswick. From this humble craft Cornelius Vanderbilt developed a fleet of freighters and then a transatlantic steamship line. In his sixties he went into railroads, and before he died this formidable old codger, who read little and could not write very well, had the satisfaction of founding a university. When he died he left his son $94,000,000, which the son doubled in ten years. The Vanderbilt house was built by the ferry-boat captain's grandson and daughter-in-law. On the shell, the house, they spent a mere $2,000,000, and $9,000,000 on the furnishings. And they opened it on a hot August night in 1892 with a ball held in a golden room such as few Newporters had ever danced in before or since. This baroque splendor produced its own baroque style of neurosis: "Nothing," a candid girl once said, "but gaiety—and grief." On a famous night, the Vanderbilt ballroom glittered with the uniforms of a historic British regiment and the decorations of the diplomatic corps. There were no soldiers or diplomats present. They were an army of actors hired by a devoted wife whose husband had gone quietly mad and believed himself to be the Prince of Wales.

The colony's houses were opened for only about seven weeks in the summer, but during that time the inmates packed a royal lifetime in formal picnics and luncheons, in dinners and polo and yachting and fancy-dress balls. It could cost up to $200,000 to throw a fancy-dress ball. There was one lady who set aside each summer $10,000 for what she would later itemize as "mistakes in my clothes." When the brother-in-law of Czar Nicholas II went to Newport, he confessed he had never even imagined such luxury. He had certainly never seen horses bedded down on linen sheets embossed with the family monogram. It was unlikely, too, that he had ever seen a man fling a Persian carpet on his lawn and order an army of gardeners to reproduce the intricacies of the pattern and colors in a mosaic of flower beds. There was a dinner at which the centerpiece was a long, thin sandbox implanted with tiny pails and shovels of sterling silver. The guests were invited on a given signal to dig for favors—for rubies, sapphires, and diamonds.

The ultimate whimsy was achieved by one Harry Lehr, an acknowledged court jester, who issued invitations to a hundred dogs and their masters. It was to be a "bow-wows' banquet." Unfortunately, a reporter had managed to crash the party, and the next morning the story went out over the wires that the banquet menu had consisted of stewed liver and rice, fricassee of bones, and shredded dog biscuit. Thanks to the telegraph and the telephone, the newspapers and then the pulpits of big and little towns throughout the country shook with warnings about the fate of Sodom and Gomorrah.

It was a bad time for such goings-on to be advertised at all outside Newport. This pitiful frivolity simply put the match to a charge that had been gathering for a decade out on the farms and the cities of the prairie. Out of a deflation through the 1880s, out of farm prices falling and credit tightening, out of strikes in steel mills and hunger riots in several cities, there arose a farmers' People's Party demanding support for their cheapened crops and the free coinage of silver. These issues might have sounded drearily academic in the East, but they were stoked with emotion by tales, true and fantastic, about the greed of the so-called Robber Barons, and the ostentation of the society they had nurtured.

And while the Newport millionaires bent for rubies with their little sterling silver shovels, children in New York bent over sewing machines sixteen hours a day, for industry had produced something that was supposed, in the not so long ago, never to happen in America—a permanent factory population. It began to see itself as the slave of the trusts and the money men. In the year that the Vanderbilts threw open their golden doors, there was a coal miners' strike, a national railroad

Like other Newport plutocrats, William K. Vanderbilt called his Marble House a "cottage". It cost $11 million to build and furnish. This is the dining room.

9

THE HUDDLED MASSES

"We call England the Mother country," Robert Benchley once remarked, "because most of us come from Poland or Italy." It's not quite as drastic as that, but today the chances of an American being of wholly English stock are, outside the South, no more than one in four. Only the English visitor is still surprised by this palpable fact. When a German makes his first trip across the Atlantic, he can go into almost any large city between southern Pennsylvania and the Great Lakes, and on across the prairie into the small towns of Kansas, and he will find himself among people whose physique is familiar, who share many of his values and his tastes in food and drink. The Scandinavian will be very much at home with the landscape and the farming of Minnesota, and he will not be surprised to hear that the state is represented in Congress by men named Langen and Olson and Nelsen. A Polish Catholic would easily pass as a native among the sandy potato fields, the lumbering wooden churches, and the Doroskis and Stepnoskis of eastern Long Island.

For three quarters of the population that hears itself so often hailed as "the American people" are the descendants of immigrants from Asia and Africa and, most of all, from the continent of Europe. They brought over with them their religions and folkways and their national foods, not least their national prejudices, which for a long time in the new country turned the cities of the Northeast and the Midwest into adjoining compounds of chauvinists, distrustful not only of immigrants from other nations everywhere but too often of their neighbors three or four blocks away.

But even the most clannish of them sooner or later had to mix with the peoples already there and learn among other things a new kind of politics, in which the dominant power went to men who knew how to balance the needs of one national group against another. The American delicatessen became an international store for the staples that the old immigrant could not do without. Few American children, certainly in the cities, need to be told that goulash comes from Hungary, liverwurst from

Aboard a ferry from Ellis Island, an Italian immigrant family gazes in hope and trepidation at the bustling reality of New York City, 1905.

Germany, borscht from Russia, and lasagne from Italy. And even Gentiles who never tasted the combination probably know that lox—smoked salmon—and the doughnut-shaped rolls called bagels are as inseparable, in Jewish households of any nationality, as an Englishman's—and an Anglo-Saxon American's—bacon and eggs.

I remember once, during a strike in New York when the salmon wasn't coming in, there seemed to be a glut of bagels in the Jewish bakeries. In a whimsical moment I sent a cable to my editor warning him that I was about to put a piece on the wire to be entitled, "Lox Lag Brings Bagel Boom." He cabled right back: "Your message hopelessly garbled it reads lox lag brings bagel boom." A small but telling sign that many Englishmen, beneath the surface admission that Americans have developed their own civilization, still think of Americans as Englishmen gone wrong. If so, the deterioration set in long ago. The American population, like the American diet, began to lose its exclusive Anglo-Saxon elements as long ago as the 1840s, with a wave of immigration that swelled to a flood, and then to a tidal wave in the thirty years between about 1885 and the First World War.

Why did they come? Why do they still come? For a mesh of reasons and impulses that condition any crucial decision in life. But the most powerful was one common to most of the immigrants from the 1840s on—hard times in the homeland. They chose America because, by the early nineteenth century, Europeans, especially if they were poor, had heard that the Americans had had a revolution that successfully overthrew the old orders of society. Madame de Staël could tell a Boston scholar, in 1817, "You are the advance guard of the human race." And Goethe, ten years later, wrote for anybody to read: "Amerika, du hast es besser als unser Kontinent" (which may be loosely translated as: "America, you have things better over there.") He was thinking of the freedom from the binding force of "useless traditions." But people who had never heard of Madame de Staël and Goethe picked up the new belief that there was a green land far away preserved "from robbers, knights and ghosts affrighting." Whenever life could hardly be worse at home, they came to believe that life was better in America.

In Ireland in the middle 1840s human life had touched bottom. Ironically, two causes of the Irish plight came *from* America. The rising competition of American agriculture made thousands of very small farmers (300,000 of Ireland's 685,000 farms had less than three acres) shift from tillage to grazing, on barren ground. And the potato blight, which was to putrefy vast harvests in a few weeks, had crossed the Atlantic from America in 1845. Within five years the potato famine had claimed almost a million Irish lives, over twenty thousand of them dropping in the fields from starvation.

The young Queen Victoria was informed that the state of Ireland was "alarming" and that the country was so full of "inflammable matter" that it could explode in rebellion. So she paid a royal visit, serenely admired the beauty of the scenery, and was relieved that the people "received us with the greatest enthusiasm." Nevertheless, at Kingston and at Cork she noted: "You see more ragged and wretched people here than I ever saw anywhere else." One of those ragged people could well have been a bankrupt farmer from Wexford County who had gone to Cork. Most such, with any energy left over after the famine, retreated to the towns and either joined sedition societies or headed for America. This one chose America, and, like very many of the Irish who came after, his destination was chosen for him by the simple fact that Boston was the end of the Cunard line. His name was Patrick Kennedy, great-grandfather of the thirty-fifth President of the United States. He was one of the 1,700,000 Irish—a little less than one quarter of the whole population when the famine began—who left for America in the 1840s and 1850s.

Hunger, then, was the spur in Ireland. There were other, equally fearful incentives. In the single year of 1848 political storms swept across Europe—in Austria, an abdication, arrests, and executions; in Italy, a revolution and a declaration of war by the Pope against Austria; in Sicily, an uprising against the King of Naples; in Germany, a liberal revolution that failed. Both then and throughout the rest of the century and on into our own, in any troubled country, whether or not its mischief could be laid to known culprits, there was always the ancient scapegoat of the Jew. In eastern and central Europe the ghettos had long been routine targets for the recruiting sergeant and the secret police, and their inhabitants were acquainted from childhood with what one of them called "the stoniest sound in the world: the midnight knock on the door." It would be hard to calculate but easy to guess at the millions of American Jews whose forefathers were harried and haunted by these persecutors. It is something hardly thought of by most of us who came here by free choice, or were born here without ever having to make a choice.

In some cities of Europe, Jews were permitted to practice their religion in compounds. But in many more places, where the Jews had been systematically vilified for fifteen hundred years, authorities considered their rituals to be as sinister as black magic, and the more daring or devout worshiped in stealth. In America, they had heard, they could worship openly in their own fashion, Orthodox, Reform, Conservative — or, as radical Reconstructionists, they could look to the United States as a permitted rallying ground on which to muster the faithful for the return to Palestine. I dwell on the Jews because, in the great tidal wave of the late nineteenth- and early twentieth-century immigration, they were

Irish immigrants disembark at the Battery in New York about 1855. The Chinese junk was the artist's invention, though a few years later a junk did visit the city.

Sooner or later, the ones with health and energy, and gumption or cunning, would want to break away altogether or at least to find some dependable link with the big alien society around them. They frequently found it in a character who haunted the docks and the employment agencies and the factories, a man whose headquarters was the local political clubhouse and whose daily beat was up and down the wobbly staircase of the tenements. The American neighborhood politician is a type not greatly admired by students of political science. Nonetheless, he was the lifeline between the castaway and the new society. In New York he was usually an Irishman or a Jew, a native American, but his parents or grandparents most likely had been immigrants, and he was well acquainted from birth with the primitive needs of people.

In exchange for your vote, a *quid pro quo* so elementary that it was only rarely hinted at, he would do his damnedest to get you a job, he would fish your son out of trouble, he would hound the landlord to repair the stove or the bathtub. You had a daughter dramatically plain—he would go to work on the marriage broker. In bad times he brought up coal and food. He knew when the baby was coming and he got the doctor. These were not casual good deeds. They were the daily grind of a system as subtle and firm as the lineaments of city geography that dictated it.

A front door was the entrance to a house of several families, and a house was connected with other houses to form a city block. So many blocks made up a precinct, serviced by political runners under a precinct captain, whose official salary was that of a fire inspector, a licensing agent of the city liquor board, or some other department of the city government. In turn, a precinct was a subdivision of a ward, patrolled by other far-ranging runners who could be brought to heel by the ward boss, the commander of the field force always in touch with other ward bosses and with such collateral officers of the dominant political party as county clerks, assessors, aldermen, state legislators, and Congressmen. The control of an election district was the prize, and the election was the payoff. From doorman to elected judge, the hierarchy of these offices was as exact as the ranks of an army—and in some cities it still is. Its responsiveness was always being tested from the top, where the ward boss might have a thousand Lithuanians dumped in his neighborhood, to the bottom, where the precinct worker or ward heeler was called on in the middle of the night to rustle up a loan, a bail bond, or a midwife.

For better or worse, it was the election district captains and the ward bosses who ran the cities. New York built the most durable (and periodically the most notorious) system in Tammany, the city's Democratic

By strength of numbers and organization, the Irish came to control the political machinery of several Eastern cities. Puck ran this cartoon in 1889.

PUCK.

10
THE PROMISE FULFILLED — THE PROMISE BROKEN

At three o'clock in the morning of Monday, November 11, 1918, the State Department announced that Germany had surrendered and signed an armistice, and that all fighting in the World War would cease at 11:00 A.M., Continental Time. The twenty-eighth President of the United States, Thomas Woodrow Wilson, a slim bespectacled man with a long jaw and the contained self-assurance of a bishop, was up and at his desk. It was the middle of the night, no time to be clacking away at his usual typewriter (though within the hour a burst of whistles and sirens and pealing bells would drown out such a scruple), so he took out a sheet of White House stationery and wrote down in pencil: "Everything for which America has fought has been accomplished. It will now be our fortunate duty to assist by example, by sober, friendly counsel, and by material aid, in the establishment of just democracy throughout the world."

It is true that the Allies could not have defeated the Central Powers without the intervention of the United States in the last eighteen months of a war which was to record an atrocious pile of casualties: more than half of Russia's mobilized twelve million were killed or wounded; five and a half of France's eight million; more than a third of the nine million recruited by the British Empire and Commonwealth; one and a half million of Italy's five and a half million. When a whole generation of Europeans was maimed and faint with exhaustion, the United States had sent into the battlefields two million brash and lusty young men. American industry, already geared to a scale of productivity that Europeans could hardly grasp, poured arms and matériel across the Atlantic. American pride in a superior technology occasionally exceeded its performance: the Germans were meant to tremble before the firm promise of thousands of airplanes, though not a single American plane arrived in France in time to be used in the war. But the rude energy of the Americans, both in the flesh and in the factory, was decisive against an

Having done their bit in what was confidently termed "the last war," the men of New York City's 165th Infantry Regiment happily arrive back home again.

303

enemy whose people were pinched by starvation, whose cavalry horses had no reserves of feed, whose military transport in the last months rode on rubberless wheels.

Undoubtedly, Europe in the flush of victory was grateful to the last and most powerful of the Allies. But neither Britain and France nor the other Allies envisioned the peace settlement quite as Woodrow Wilson led the American people to see it, as a kind of moral Olympiad at which the United States would be the host nation. Soon after the Armistice, President Wilson began to draft in his mind a grand plan for "the establishment of just democracy throughout the world." The presumption of his rhetoric spread beyond the White House. "Now that the forces of Right have begun their reconstruction of humanity's morals," a newspaper proclaimed in November 1918, "the world faces a material task of equal magnitude." This purple passage came from an advertisement for steel window frames.

Between Wilson's self-assigned mission to preside over the peace and the advertising copywriter's celebration of America's industrial prowess, there is a link of moral and material pride that recalls the most rooted beliefs of the founders of New England: that a good Puritan, though living a life of the strictest piety, must yet live in the world and make God's will work through government, that material success or failure is not an aim in itself but a proof of God's pleasure. Now that America had saved old Europe, America would "reconstruct humanity's morals" and incidentally create unprecedented wealth. The twentieth century was to fulfill the promise of the Puritan fathers that goodness and success go hand in hand. And, so it seemed in 1919, America could not have had more providential luck than to find Woodrow Wilson in the White House. He was the perfect prototype of the seventeenth-century Puritan reincarnated. He would have been old John Winthrop's choice—and, with becoming modesty, his own—for President of the United States, if not of the world.

He was born in Virginia in 1856 and was steeped in Presbyterian blood down many generations, out of Scotland on the one side and Ulster on the other. His father was a Presbyterian minister, the son's lifelong model for high thinking and plain living. Moving from manse to manse, young Woodrow spent his boyhood in Georgia and South Carolina. From his earliest years, he was plainly intended to be a scholar, and he moved sedately down the groves of academe until, in his forty-sixth year, he became president of Princeton. His lectures, buoyant with high-toned and uplifting passages about corruption in government and greed in big business, were frequently published in magazines as philippics against Congress and the trusts.

But until he was fifty-five years old, which in 1911 was practically the twilight years, he was a theoretician. Then he was chosen by the Democratic bosses of New Jersey for the governorship as a highly respectable front—until he got to the governor's mansion and pained them with a state primary law, an employers' liability act, and other fumigating reforms. Within the year he had the luck to appeal to the elders of his party when they were more interested in defeating a Tammany-backed man for President than nominating their own. He would have had little chance of election if Theodore Roosevelt had not bolted the Republican party and set up his own, thereby splitting the Republican vote and permitting Wilson to walk serenely through the middle and become, two years after leaving Princeton, President of the United States.

There are three things about Woodrow Wilson that elevated him, for a dizzy year or so, to the status of a world savior, and in the end they brought him down: his unwavering high moral tone, his self-intoxicating eloquence, and his true concern for the dispossessed. From his college days on he saw himself as at least a favorite pupil of God, retained an absolute confidence in his own moral principles, and held a collateral belief that compromise is moral treason. Secondly, he was able to convey through the cloudy grandeur of his speeches, most of all when Americans were in the first flush of victory, the conviction that his righteous feelings were theirs.

The third thing was as rooted in his childhood as his piety but did him, in my opinion, a good deal more credit. He was nine years old when the Civil War ended, and he grew up in a wasteland of impoverished Southerners being treated as beaten aliens in their own country. When the World War was over, he was genuinely moved by the similar plight, on a huger scale, of the broken countries of central Europe. Then, as in an Old Testament dream, he had a revelation. He would go to Europe not simply as the chief American representative at the peace conference gathering in Versailles. He would draft, and hope to dictate, a new world order under a League of Nations pledged to universal peace. He would give to all small countries the right to govern themselves, "the right of self-determination." As he sailed for France, in December 1918, the first President to leave the country while in office, he said: "We are to be an instrument in the hands of God to see that liberty is made secure for mankind."

Also aboard was Robert Lansing, the Secretary of State. He confided to his journal: "The more I think about the President's declaration as to the right of 'self-determination,' the more convinced I am [that] . . . it is bound to be the basis of impossible demands on the Peace Conference . . . what misery it will cause." Lansing mooted his misgivings to

American painter George Luks saw Armistice Night, 1918, as an enormous outburst of flags, fireworks, and public enthusiasm.

Wilson, who coldly replied that it would not be a peace of "legalisms."

Wilson's vision had floated ahead of him to Europe, and to the dazzled crowds in Paris his coming was like the entry into Jerusalem. No President, no statesman of any country, had been so received as the deliverer who would lead us all into the promised land.

The disillusion in him was swift, and it came first in private to the Allied statesmen—to Lloyd George, Clemenceau, and Orlando, and their aides—who had expected a statesman and encountered a divine. It is not difficult to imagine the effect of this character, sitting coolly in the cloister of his own righteousness, on statesmen passionately drawing new frontiers, adjudicating the claims of millions of nationals for larger homelands, negotiating customs agreements, saying which country should control a river or a railway system, distributing the loser's colonies, most of all trying to thrash their way through the monstrous complexity of Europe's ethnic and nationalist jealousies, which a simpler offer of "self-determination" would only confuse rather than placate. At the end of it, the language of the treaty was artfully dressed up to hide from the President the honest realities he could not acknowledge, such as the French desire for some limits to the population of Germany and some economic restraints on her power to make another war. Wilson was placated by the smooth ambiguities of a super-subtle treaty. And he relaxed the one moral stand that reflected his courage: his steady suspicion that Germany was being asked to pay back, one way and another, more money than she could ever earn.

Wilson sailed for home amid a bedlam of criticism. The French press thought him pro-German. The British deplored his vague self-righteousness and lack of practicality. All the Allies began to fear, correctly, that they would be unable to repay the huge sums the United States had loaned them. (By 1967, fifty years after the United States had entered the war, France's original debt of just over 4.0 billion (i.e. 4,000 million) dollars had risen with unpaid interest to over 5.0 billion; Great Britain's 4.8 billion-dollar indebtedness was now at 7.3 billion, an interesting and forgotten figure never likely to be expunged from the books.)

Wilson received a formal welcome when he sailed into New York, but the domestic disillusion with him was cruelly swift. The Congress had no sure knowledge but a number of sharp suspicions about how much American sovereignty had been traded away to Wilson's precious League of Nations. The Senate would in time reject the Covenant of the League and so deliver the first world organization a body blow in its cradle.

While still president of Princeton University and not yet a politician, Woodrow Wilson sat stiffly for a portrait on the lawn of "Prospect," his home.

But "internationalism" had taken on an uglier popular meaning. It came to signify "international Communism," which had already over-thrown imperial Russia and terrified her neighbors. Within ten days of the Armistice, bands of soldiers broke up a Socialist rally in Madison Square Garden, and the next night a meeting of people who dared to call themselves "sympathizers" with the Russian Revolution was dispersed after some bloody beatings. While Wilson was at his lofty bargaining in Paris, the country was seized with the fear that the last great wave of immigrants had brought the revolutionary infection with them. Few ironies of the American experience are so exquisite or so sour as the predicament, in the dreadful year of 1919, of an American fresh from the battlefields of Europe—some soldier named, say, Polanski or Steinberg—who had once fled from persecution in the old country and was now persecuted in the new as a Bolshevik.

Every misfortune that normally follows in the train of a great war—the closing of munitions factories, a cutback in the working week, a slump in the price of crops that for four years had poured into the granaries of the Allies—could be interpreted as tactical triumphs of the Communist strategy to overthrow the American republic. The Mayor of Seattle, a stronghold of the radical Industrial Workers of the World and the scene of a city strike, received a bomb in the mail. So, in Atlanta, did the chairman of the Senate's Immigration Committee. The first law officer of the United States, the Attorney General himself, had his house in Washington blown up. He was A. Mitchell Palmer, a confessed Quaker but probably the most belligerent Quaker in the history of the faith.

Palmer's name should be memorized in schools as the archetype of the paranoid witch hunter with which the Republic is regularly afflicted whenever an unpleasant turn of history—a spy scare, a wave of violence, a dramatic plunge of the stock market, the "loss" of some foreign ally we never owned—cannot be logically explained or seems to be beyond the control of the government of the United States. He ordered or con-doned raids on magazine offices, public halls, private houses, union headquarters, meetings big and small of anyone—socialists, liberals, atheists, freethinkers, social workers—who could be identified or accused as Bolsheviks or rumored to be such by the nearest excitable citizen. Palmer's hysterical example led, among other horrors, to a drastic revision of the immigration laws. The flow of immigrants from eastern and southern Europe slowed to a dribble, and there was a time when more people were being deported from Ellis Island than were coming in. In the South and Midwest, the chauvinist fever took a virulent form all too common among Anglo-Saxons and Celts when they are touched by panic: it bred a bigot army, led by the Ku Klux Klan, dedicated to the harassment, beating, and occasional lynching of any "foreigner" who could not claim Anglo-Saxon Christian origins, that is to say the Jew, the Roman Catholic, and the Negro.

The returned soldiers and the released munitions workers had their legitimate grievances and added them to the general ferment. Veterans had been promised homes and found surburban boxes at extravagant rents. During the war, labor had willingly forfeited the right to strike. Now it was freed from that pledge, and its instinct, in the face of arbitrary layoffs and an alarming rise in the cost of living, was to strike. In 1919, one of the black years of this century, there was a national steel strike and a railroad strike and a police strike in Boston and race riots in twenty-three cities. For there was a new menace to the city worker's peace of mind—the black man and his family from the South, who had moved into the Northern industrial towns to do war work, and when the war was over stayed housed in what had once been lower-middle-class white neighborhoods.

In July 1919 a teen-aged black boy—"colored," as we should have called him then—was holding on to a railroad tie after a bout of swimming in Lake Michigan when he happened to drift over to the waters facing a beach reserved for whites. He was stoned from the white beach. Soon afterwards he was seen to lose his grip of the tie. Nobody ever knew for certain whether he had been hit, but he drowned—and his friends back on the black beach stormed over to the whites. This was the start of a riot that seized all the neighborhoods where Negroes had moved into the white fringes. For one week Chicago was a battleground for bombings, shootings, stabbings, fires, white forays into Negro slums, gang retaliations; and at the end of it twenty-three Negroes and fifteen whites were dead, and five hundred thirty-seven people were wounded.

A small footnote to the history of idealism is the fact that, throughout Attorney General Palmer's notorious "raids," throughout the sickness and violence of 1919, Wilson had only one thing in mind: to see the Treaty of Versailles passed unimpaired by the Senate. While the Senate was hedging the treaty with reservations that would exclude the United States from the League of Nations, Wilson resolved to talk the people into it. While in the Rockies, however, his health broke, and his train came home. He suffered a cerebral thrombosis and for seventeen months he lay or dozed in the White House, a sick shadow of the savior of Europe, quite beyond the management of his office.

He was not removed for disability. He was charitably ignored. Americans were already bored or disenchanted with Europe, a Europe haggling

Overleaf: *Lynch law flourished in the years after World War I; in 1919 alone, 70 Negroes were lynched. This grisly scene took place in Marion, Indiana in August, 1930.*

311

Sears, Roebuck and Co., Chicago

Spring and Summer - 1927

Index and Information Pages - 459 to 485

were wearing in New York and Chicago. And for ninety-five cents, her daughter could get the very hat that was worn by the "It Girl," Clara Bow, one of the first idols of the motion picture industry, which was beginning to serve a collateral function as the national store window for fashions of all sorts—bathing suits and hairdos and furniture and the cocktail habit and "companionate marriage" and many other fads and frivolities.

Hollywood grew to be the most flourishing factory of popular mythology since the Greeks. It is the main reason why the America of the 1920s that passed into the file of the world's memory is not an America of throbbing steel production, not the sudden flowering of a brilliant native literature, but a kind of mass idiocy and frivolity. Europe, drained of life and invention after the war, first jeered and then eagerly copied these hectic fads—cocktails, bobbed hair, the Charleston, and night clubs, and also the lyrical tunes of Richard Rodgers, the love-lorn waltzes of Irving Berlin, the bounce and poignancy of George Gershwin—as new signs of life.

America was top dog and knew it and was consumed with an itch for the superlative. Even so austere a figure as Justice Oliver Wendell Holmes sensed the mood at the end of the World War and generalized in a learned article on natural law what was to become a law of competitive life for Americans in the 1920s:

It is not enough for the knight of romance that you agree that his lady is a very nice girl—if you do not admit that she is the best God ever made or will make, you must fight. There is in all men a demand for the superlative, so much so that the poor devil who has no other way of reaching it attains it by getting drunk.

America had attained it by making Wall Street the world's money mart, and Hollywood the factory of the world's daydreams, and Tin Pan Alley the maker of the music it danced to. It seemed only right and proper that the first mother to swim the English Channel should be an American mother.

Given the national mood, it was only appropriate that suddenly, in 1927, the overnight hero of the world was an American. On a drizzly May morning, an airplane lined up on a muddy, primitive runway on Long Island. It was going for a shot at a $25,000 prize for a nonstop transatlantic flight. Of the three contenders, this was both the strangest and the smallest: it was twenty-seven feet, eight inches long, had no radio and no sextant, and its instrument panel was only a little more pretentious than that of a 1927 automobile. It had cost $10,580, and every inch of its construction had been watched over by the man who was going to fly it; unlike the others he was going alone, and he did not intend to hop islands or countries, he was going for the whole stretch—New York to

By 1927 the Sears, Roebuck catalogue was running to nearly 1,100 pages containing "35,000 Bargains," and the company's sales exceeded $300 million a year. To customers and would-be customers, the catalogue was "The Great Wish Book."

319

At Long Island's Roosevelt Field, Charles Lindbergh stands beneath the wing of his monoplane. At right, New York welcomes him home with ticker-tape.

Paris. He was a skinny, blond twenty-five-year-old from Minnesota, who had been a parachute jumper and an airmail pilot in the wildcat days.

The plane—which for balance carried all the gasoline it could in a cased-in cockpit up front, so that the pilot was literally flying blind—wobbled and bounced into the heavy skies, and that night forty thousand boxing fans in New York stood and prayed for its pilot. In Tokyo, at their midnight, people swarmed into the streets. The stock exchanges of London, Berlin, and Amsterdam interrupted regular quotations with the word—that there was no word. As the second night came on in Paris, an appeal went out to everybody who owned an automobile—which might be from seventy to eighty thousand, maybe—to head for a landing field at Le Bourget and line up in two files, switch the headlights on and thus create a visible shaft of white fog. Into it, thirty-three hours after just missing the telephone wires on Long Island, the strange plane trundled and stopped. It was engulfed by one hundred thousand Parisians. When they lifted the pilot out of the cockpit, if he had said he was Alexander the Great, they'd have believed him. He reportedly said simply: "I am Charles Lindbergh." He came home to naval salutes and a frenetic press, and a ticker-tape parade up Broadway.

The ticker-tape parade was to become New York's special accolade for a few carefully chosen national gods. Down the decades the biggest blizzards have been reserved for such returning heroes as General Eisenhower, General MacArthur, astronaut John Glenn, and, three years after Lindbergh, a sunny, firm-jawed, handsome lawyer from Atlanta, Georgia. A peculiar choice, but in him the 1920s was saluting an old ideal in the moment of its passing.

He was Robert Tyre Jones, Jr., a weekend golfer but the best golfer of his time, some people think the best of all time. But he had a grace and charm on and off the course that, curiously, made him the idol of two continents in a very brash time, and that to people who didn't know a putter from a shovel. His universal appeal was not as a golfer. What then? The word that comes to mind is an extinct word: a gentleman, a combination of goodness and grace, an unwavering courtesy, self-deprecation, and consideration for other people. This fetching combination, allied to his world supremacy in one sport, was what made him a hero in Scotland and England as much as in the Midwest and his native Georgia.

Once, in a national championship, he drove his ball into the woods. He went after it alone, and, in standing to the ball, he barely touched it. He came out of the woods, signaled his fault, penalized himself one stroke and by one stroke lost the championship. When he was praised for this and similar acts of sportsmanship, he was genuinely disgusted. "You might as well," he said, "praise a man for not robbing a bank."

In his middle forties he was paralyzed by a rare disease, and a friend asked him for the medical outlook. "I will tell you privately," he said, "it's not going to get better, it's going to get worse all the time, but don't fret. Remember, we 'play the ball where it lies,' and now let's not talk about this, ever again." And he never did. So what we're talking about is not the hero as golfer but something that America hungered for and found: the best performer in the world who was also the hero as human being, the gentle, chivalrous, wholly self-sufficient male. Jefferson's lost paragon, the wise innocent.

Innocence was something that most mothers wished very much their daughters had. For the 1920s brought on a drastic revolt against the prewar mores of gentility; and though the revolutionary symbols now seem trivial, they were sufficiently bizarre to alarm the middle-aged. Corsets were abandoned along with the Viennese waltz. Long skirts were scandalously abbreviated, and long hair was "bobbed." Young women smoked, and in public, and danced into the dawn to the sensual moan of the saxophone, an instrument forgotten for eighty years but now revived and condemned, by city fathers and magistrates on both sides of the Atlantic, as a siren sound beckoning young girls to a losing battle with a fate worse than death.

Not all of the parental anxiety was misplaced. Sexual "emancipation" was the watchword of the young, and it was lent a frightening authority by Dr. Sigmund Freud, whose theory and practice of psychoanalysis became a daring fashion. Not from Freud himself but from brisk newspaper and magazine popularizations, both young and old picked up a grotesque misunderstanding of Freud's theory of unconscious repression: which is what happens when people repress an instinct and don't know they're doing it. What everybody seemed to think he was saying was that consciously to *suppress* an instinct, any instinct, would make you break out in insanity or pimples. So sex drenched the magazines and the movies and the theater, until Robert Benchley, the drama critic of *The New Yorker*, was driven to write:

I am now definitely ready to announce that Sex, as a theatrical property, is as tiresome as the Old Mortgage . . . I am sick of rebellious youth and I'm sick of Victorian parents and I don't care if all the little girls in all sections of the United States get ruined, or want to get ruined, or keep from getting ruined. All I ask is: don't write plays about it and ask me to sit through them.

There was something worse than the saxophone or bobbed hair, if not sex, because it stimulated every vice—liquor, whose very illegality made it as precious as forbidden fruit. In the moral fervor of the First World War, Congress had passed a Constitutional Amendment that long-suffering wives of drunken husbands on the frontier had been demanding for half a century: the total national prohibition of the manufacture, transportation, and sale of alcohol. When the war was over, it was backed by law, and it was subsequently known as the Noble Experiment. It did not noticeably endow Americans with more nobility than they already had. On the contrary, it gave rise to a national underground industry, based in Chicago, that turned small-time safecrackers and brothel owners into millionaires.

Gangsters were not new in America, but Prohibition opened up the green pastures to men who organized their own breweries and transport, paid off the police, supplied rot-gut liquor to hand-picked clubs, and stuck the owners with a further protection fee in case, as occasionally happened, some underpaid police squad might forget itself and enforce the law. In time the gang leaders grew greedy, divided Chicago into rival territories, and fought each other for their control. But, in accordance with the old Roman code, they showed resolution in war and magnanimity in victory. There was, for instance, Dion O'Banion, an Irishman whose cover for his liquor empire was a florist's shop. He was double-crossed by an Italian, made a derisory remark about Sicilians, and was successfully disposed of by Al Capone and Johnny Torrio. His funeral casket was of bronze and solid silver. It was followed by the sorrowful Capone and Torrio, and by $50,000 worth of flowers contributed, in loving memory, by the opposition. The murderers were never found. Capone, however, had the sense to buy himself an armor-plated Cadillac.

The conspicuous gangsters of the 1920s have vanished. In our time, they have moved with masterly discretion into real estate, banking, the export-import trade in drugs, the control of supermarkets, hotels, big and little corporations—so that today nobody knows for sure where legitimate business ends and the syndicate takes over.

It took America thirteen years to concede that the Noble Experiment was a squalid disaster. While it flourished, the public momentarily shuddered at the gangland murders and the baroque funerals, then returned to its pleasures and its prosperity. These Chicago episodes were mere excrescences on the general health. A good man was in the White House, and business was booming. Church membership in the United States had never been higher, and the pulpits resounded with some of Winthrop's favorite texts: "Thou shalt remember the Lord thy God, for it is He that giveth thee the power to get wealth" . . . . "Blessed is the man that feareth the Lord . . . . His seed shall be mighty upon earth . . . . wealth and riches shall be in his house."

Some explanation of these providential blessings had to be found, and it came from another Chicagoan, appropriately a parson's son, who had

The best thing about Prohibition may have been its end. In 1933, a group of young ladies celebrated repeal for the benefit of a news photographer.

helped to found a giant advertising company. His name was Bruce Barton, and he wrote a book called *The Man Nobody Knows*. It could have carried the subtitle "The Puritan Promise Fulfilled." It sold close to a million. Like popular mystics before and since, Barton re-created God in the image of his time. He took a second look at the Carpenter of Nazareth and saw him as Jesus Christ, Supersalesman. From the book we learn that Jesus was an advertising genius and that copywriters would do well to copy the pith of his slogans: "Arise, take up thy bed and walk"; "What shall it profit a man if he gain the whole world and lose his own soul?"; "Render unto Caesar the things that are Caesar's." In another chapter, we learn also that Jesus was the founder of modern business, having taken "twelve men from the bottom ranks of business and forged them into an organization that conquered the world." Above all, says Barton, He made no distinction between business and "my Father's business." That is to say, between work and religion. And neither did Calvin Coolidge.

Did Coolidge have some foreboding of what was going to happen to this earthly paradise? He gave no hint of it. Nevertheless, in the spring of 1928 he abruptly announced that he was not going to run again for the Presidency. "There was a volcano boiling under him," wrote H. L. Mencken, "but he did not know it, and was not singed. When it burst forth at last, it was Hoover who got its blast, and was fried, boiled, roasted and fricasseed."

The volcano erupted on the floor of the New York Stock Exchange and burned corporations, banks, taxi drivers, farmers, janitors, and chorus girls, all those who had been riding high in what President Hoover had called "the final triumph over poverty." On October 24, 1929, blocks of shares went down the river in ten- and twenty-thousand lots. Five days later came the deluge, and it became clear years too late that the torrent of liquidation was caused, not so much by the big traders and bankers—who rushed in to try and plug the flood with twenty-five million dollars—but by legions of small-timers who had no margins to speak of. In other words, the Everest of the 1929 stock market was a mountain of credit on a molehill of actual money. Now, to the very Puritans who had seen the hand of God in the Coolidge prosperity, the crash was a punishment; and the pulpits now groaned with other, forgotten warnings from the Psalms: "They that trust in their wealth, and boast themselves in the multitude of their riches; none of them can by any means redeem his brother, nor give to God a ransom for him."

Other, more secular analysts saw—though admittedly by hindsight —other explanations. Today you cannot buy without meeting high margin requirements. In 1929 you could buy a dollar stock with ten cents in your hand; today it would have to be sixty to sixty-five cents. The federal government regulates investing, and insures brokerage accounts, as it also insures the smallest bank deposit. But none of these safeguards existed in the 1929 casino of the stock market. And the weekly theatrical trade journal *Variety* summed it up in five grim, sassy words: "Wall Street Lays An Egg."

Nowhere, in the following months and years, was the going so rough as in the idle factories, for this nation had been the first to transfer skill on a massive scale from the man to the machine. Yet, within three months of the crash, men who worked in big factories, small men who had merrily played the market, were warming their hands before scrap wood fires in the underpass beneath the Chicago Opera House (Samuel Insull, the man who had made a present of it to the city, saw some hungry and muttering mobs and quietly increased his bodyguard from two to thirty). But the Great Depression in America was not just a blow to the extremes of the millionaire and the coal miner. It blighted everybody, except the very poor who had nothing to lose. When steel stocks went from ninety down to twelve, the automobile manufacturers simply let half their workers go. There were skyscrapers just finished that lacked tenants. A secretary was a ridiculous luxury. There were truckers with nothing to truck, crops that went unharvested, milk that went undelivered to people who couldn't afford it. When I first arrived here, as a student in a college town, I couldn't go out in the evening to mail a letter without being stopped by nicely dressed men who had told their wives they were out looking for night work. So they were—they were out on the streets cadging dimes and quarters.

Somebody had to take the blame, and it fell on Coolidge's unlucky successor, President Herbert Clark Hoover, a world-famous engineer who had done mighty work ten years earlier organizing the feeding of starving Europe. He had been at Versailles, where John Maynard Keynes had called him the only man there who "imported into the councils of Paris . . . precisely that atmosphere of reality, knowledge, magnanimity and disinterestedness which, if they had been found in other quarters also, would have given us the Good Peace." But now Hoover was simply the football coach whose plays lost the big game, and his bitter memorial was the shanty towns of the unemployed down by the rivers of scores of cities.

Outside the cities were the bankrupt farmers who had fed the armies of Europe in the fat years and had known only collapsing prices ever since. (Harry Truman's Kansas City haberdashery went bust not in 1929 but in 1922, when "90 cent wheat would not buy $15 shirts.") The farmers had been the forgotten men of the Coolidge prosperity. The rural South had been forgotten or exploited since the Civil War and had overplowed its cotton land for generations till the topsoil crumbled and the hillsides were trenched with erosion. Out on the prairie and the Great Plains beyond, an unending drought through the mid-1930s and the steady west wind withered the wheatlands and buried farms to their windowsills in oceans of sand. And when, during two summers, the western sky billowed with the terrifying "black rollers," the farmers saw the punishment of the Old Testament God in "the whirlwind by day and the darkness at noon."

Long before the drought and the Dust Bowl, and long ignored by the prospering cities, was the nation's chronic poor relation—the South. For three quarters of a century Southern tenant farmers, white and black, had been very sad citizens, the victims of worn-out single crops, living off a diet of corn, fatback pork, and no green vegetables. They were not, as the Northern press made them out to be, shiftless people; they were exhausted from the twin diseases of malnutrition: scurvy, and pellagra.

Perhaps more than the rest of us, they were to find their redeemer in a man who lived a thousand miles away from them, and a million light-years from their experience of the life and death of an American family. He was the thirty-second President of the United States, the luckless Hoover's Democratic successor: Franklin Delano Roosevelt, mostly of English blood with a dash of Dutch. His father, already over fifty when the boy was born, was a dim, genteel country squire of substantial means. His mother was an adoring, imperious matriarch, who would surely have agreed with George Bernard Shaw: "Never fret for an only son, the idea of failure will never occur to him." It was a highly cushioned life young Roosevelt led in his birthplace, a two-winged Hudson River "bracketed villa" (later done over as a Georgian stone mansion) ninety miles north of New York City with a noble prospect over the river. Here Franklin Roosevelt led a charmed life, and all through his life he was a charmer. His mother didn't want to have him coarsened by contact with a rabble of other boys, so she brought in private tutors until he was ready for Groton. He wasn't much of a student but, being mad for boats, dabbled a little in naval history. (If the navy had been at the disposal of his mother, she would have given it to him for Christmas.)

After Groton he ambled socially through Harvard, married the niece of the former Republican President, Theodore Roosevelt, and then went to law school. He never graduated, but through his connections joined a prosperous law firm, got into politics, and in the First World War wangled the only job he wanted, Assistant Secretary of the Navy. In 1920 the glamour of the Roosevelt name was appropriated by the Democrats, and they ran him for Vice-President. He was buried in the Harding landslide, along with the other apostles of Woodrow Wilson, but twelve years later he was resurrected as a presidential candidate. He might be Governor of New York, but he was not the most acceptable

White House material. It was a heavy handicap for an American politician to have gone to Harvard and have an upper-crust accent. And there was another political liability: he was a mother's boy from the landed gentry. To compound his disabilities, he had been paralyzed by poliomyelitis in his fortieth year, and for the rest of his life he never had the use of his legs. Yet, throughout the twelve years of his Presidency, the press, including the inveterate smart alecks among the still and newsreel photographers, respected a convention unlikely to be honored today: they never photographed him in movement. I saw him once being lifted out of his car like a sack of potatoes, and put on his feet, and given two sticks and two helping hands, and his hat stuck on his head for him. This was not the Roosevelt the public saw. They saw the burly upper body, the bull-like neck, and the tossing head, the confident savior of the Republic in a dark time.

He was elected President in 1932 (not to mention 1936, 1940, and 1944, the only man to break the record of two terms in the White House). In the month before his inauguration, banks were failing every hour, and for two weeks gold and currency were being withdrawn at the appalling rate of $15,000,000 a day. The government, which had lent over $850,000,000 to the banks, now started to lend heavily to the railroads. On March 4, 1933, the day of his inauguration, Roosevelt hurled a thunderbolt at the headlines by closing—without any sure legal sanction—every bank in the country. He would decide which banks deserved federal support and which would have to go under. It was the day the money stopped; literally, you had to cadge a meal, live on the tab in places that knew you, pay with a check for a cab ride and once—I remember—for a shoeshine.

Roosevelt then asked Congress for emergency power "as great as the power that would be given me if we were in fact invaded by a foreign foe." Since there were twelve or thirteen million unemployed, he got it. Congress passed the legislation and he proclaimed something called the NRA (the National Recovery Administration), which practically appropriated the lawmaking power of Congress, suspended antitrust laws and sanctioned government by trade association by requiring employers to draw up a binding code affecting about seven hundred industries, fixing wages and prices and labor practices for everybody from steelworkers to burlesque strippers.

Roosevelt, having promised to give the government back to the states, had seized power at the center. For two dizzy years, America had a fling at National Socialism. Roosevelt was for all administrative purposes a dictator, but a benevolent one, and the country loved it. In time, however, it became too much for the "nine old men" of the Supreme Court. As so often happens with the Court, it took only a tiny pretext to destroy

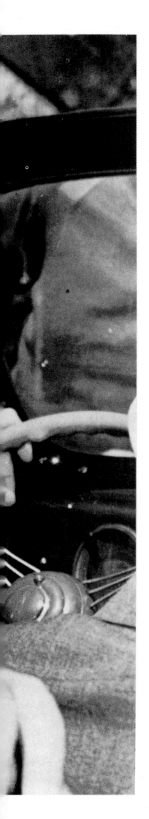

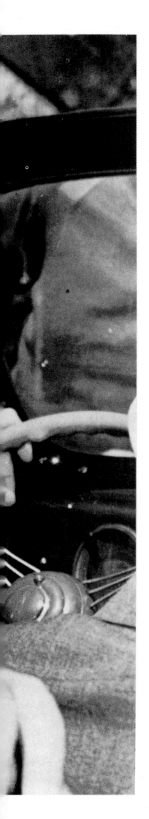

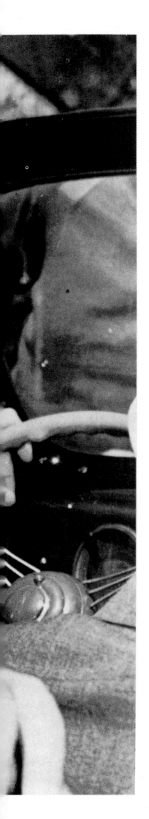

h

a mighty power. In a decisive case the Court ruled that, if two brothers reared a sick chicken in New York State and sold it there, it was no business of the executive branch of the federal government—that, in short, the whole NRA "code" had stolen the constitutional lawmaking power from the Congress. The NRA was destroyed. Roosevelt fumed, but only for a while, because he was never down for long. He returned to his great gift for directing the gaze of the lawmakers at the dire plight of the whole continent, and Congress disbursed relief funds in floods. He had in the meantime shoved through Congress huge federal loans for public works, and at the same time he gave the industrial worker who had been hounded by company spies the right to organize and bargain. He handed out hard dollars to the unemployed and took three million youngsters off the streets to build highways and plant ten million trees. He mobilized actors in a federal theater and, in the happiest inspiration of the Works Progress Administration, hired unemployed scholars, writers, and local historians to produce several hundred volumes of guidebooks to the states. He stopped the automatic production of groaning farm surpluses, paid the Southern farmers to diversify their crops and built enormous dams to hold the flooding of the great river valleys—and then made the valleys flower through electricity and controlled irrigation. In all, he brought national relief to national unemployment; he conserved the soil of the worn-out South; he established once for all the federal government's right to plan economic and social welfare on a national scale, as the great corporations had done for their industries; he captured the ruling initiative from Congress and, like no President since Wilson, used the Presidency as the spokesman of the people's needs.

In effect, he signed a check in the government's name for several billion invisible dollars. What strikes me about him now is the triumphant contradiction between his genial, fluty manner and his extraordinary tough hide. He would make up to anyone he needed, a labor leader in one state, a conservative Republican in another. He would overlook the race bigotry of a Senator in a Southern state where he wanted to do something for the poor white farmers. And on behalf of what he called first "the forgotten man" and then "the little man," he allied himself with corrupt city governments, in Memphis, Jersey City, Chicago, because —as he once privately said—"they may be sons of bitches but they are our sons of bitches." Not since Lincoln had there been such an artful manipulator of the good, the bad, and the bewildered in between. I believe he saved the capitalist system by deliberately forgetting to bal-

With a cigarette holder at its customarily jaunty angle, Franklin Delano Roosevelt was photographed in 1939 in his hand-controlled Ford coupé.

ance the books, by transferring the gorgeous resources of credit from the bankers to the government, no matter what the national debt might be. A journalist of ferocious talent, Westbrook Pegler, who loathed Roosevelt for most of his later days, has written, I believe, his best epitaph:

As a social and political liver-shaker he has had no equal in our time in this country. Ornery, tricky, stubborn, wayward and strong as a bull.... He looked nice and dressy back there in 1932 ... there was nothing in his past record to indicate what a cantankerous hide he would turn out to be.... Anyone who gentles Mr. Roosevelt is simply imposing a handicap on himself, for he won't gentle you back.... But never in our time have people been so conscious of the meanness which a complacent upper class will practice on the help, and of the government's duty to do something real and personal for the assistance of those who are so far down that they can't help themselves. He needs to be fought all the time, for he has an enormous appreciation of himself and of any idea which he happens to approve, but if the country doesn't go absolutely broke in his time, it will be a more intelligent and a better country after him.

Yet Roosevelt came in on a promise to do something that has balked governments of every ideological brand before and since—to guarantee full employment in peacetime. He didn't make it. In 1938 there were still ten million unemployed. In the next four years the number did indeed shrink—it went out of sight—but this was not Roosevelt's doing but Hitler's. Because the stacks of the steel mills barely began to belch smoke again until the first war orders came in from the British and the French.

The American artist Thomas Hart Benton began his mural, "America Today," in 1930, on a wall at the New School in New York. This panel is "The Changing West."

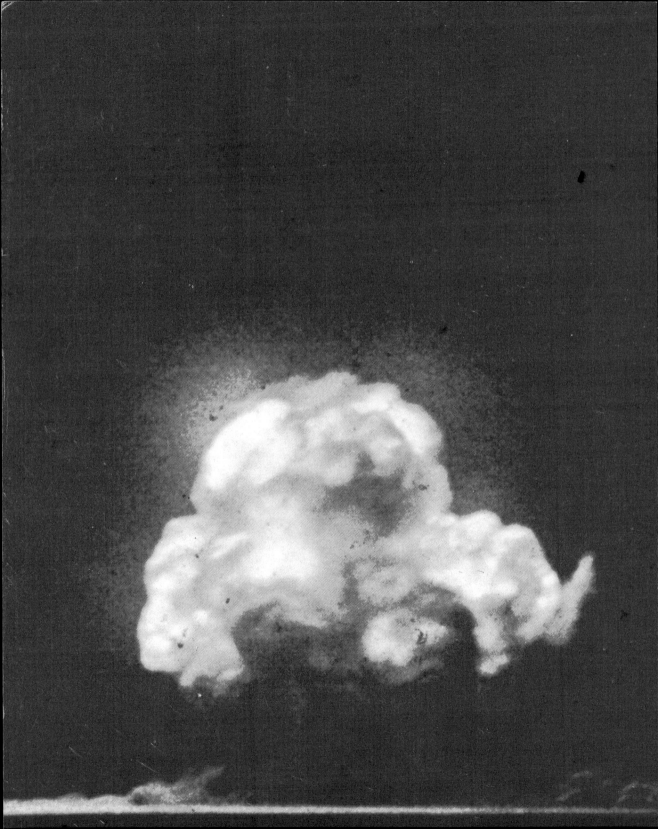

ments and President Truman's civil rights campaign in the election of 1948.

But 1954 was the year that sparked the black revolution of our day, and the innocents who lit the charge were Oliver Brown, of Topeka, Kansas, and his eight-year-old daughter, in whose behalf the father sued the city school board for forbidding her to go to a white school a few blocks away, forcing her instead to cross railroad yards to take a bus twenty-one blocks away. The Supreme Court ruled in her favor, overthrew the Plessy doctrine of sixty-two years before, declared that to separate whites and blacks in public education deprived children of "the equal protection of the laws guaranteed by the Fourteenth Amendment," and ordered the integration of public schools "with all deliberate speed." The majority opinion was written by Chief Justice Earl Warren, whom President Eisenhower had appointed to the Court in the awareness that he had once been a genial, sound, conservative old district attorney. The apotheosis of Earl Warren was something that baffled Eisenhower till the day he died.

For several years the Southern legislatures wriggled through a mesh of loopholes in their state constitutions to reassert the right of segregation. And since "deliberate speed" moved no faster than a turtle, the Negroes began their own mass protests, against many of the old offenses, first with laborious marches in the company of white sympathizers. Everyone anticipated trouble in the South, and that's where the first sporadic violence came. But no one guessed at the tenacious resistance of the whites in the cities of the North. The word "confrontation" emerged from the dictionary with a new and menacing air—in Little Rock, Arkansas; in Oxford, Mississippi; in Dallas, Texas; in Watts, California; in Detroit, Newark, Baltimore, and Washington. The subsequent turmoil is a part of all our lives.

Today the mass of blacks is not much better off, except —surprisingly —in local government in small Southern towns. Yet on college campuses and in training schools, there are blacks learning professions and businesses that they will practice in the white world. There are blacks who want no part of the white world, who want a black Establishment, even lands or separate states of their own. And there are blacks who want any number of alternatives in between.

In the universities, schools of African studies are reteaching the history of America and erecting a pantheon of forgotten heroes—Nat Turner, a Virginia slave who led an insurrection and was hanged in 1831; Marcus Garvey, a Jamaican who started a Negro nationalist movement in New York in 1917 to develop independent Negro nations in Africa and who was jailed for supposedly misusing the funds subscribed for the steamship line that would carry the colonizers back to Africa—and contemporaries who were to turn into murdered martyrs, Malcolm X and Martin Luther King. For the first time the black population of America, the submerged one ninth, has developed a philosophy and is acting on it. In 1972 the first wholly black political convention was held. But however much we may feel that the violence of the 1960s is a terror that has passed, the pressures that sparked it are with us still.

Speaking for myself, I believe that Monroe's and Garvey's solution—which Lincoln approved with wistful hindsight—might have been wise in 1820. But it is a century and a half too late. I do not know what the realistic solution is. I do know (and there are many disenchanting episodes in American history to prove it) that few things are more mischievous to good government and to "domestic tranquillity" than splendid rhetoric that doesn't pay off. There is certainly the smell of such rhetoric in the Establishment's reassurances and also in what the active majority of black leaders are asking: the rehousing of one ninth of the population; the chance of free education through college; the strangling of the international and national drug traffic at its roots; a radical integration of the police forces; and the overhauling of the prisons, the jury system, and the courts. This is no more than standard liberal, even conservative libertarian, doctrine, but it would call for prodigies of goodwill. It would also call for a massive subsidy of taxes, white taxes, beyond the experience or the known tolerance of the whites to bear.

As a historian I'm not sure that an integrated society will work. As an old reporter I suspect that the blacks will not get more than Lincoln's "mass of whites" is willing to give them. The best hope, the only sensible hope, is that the mass of whites have greatly changed since Lincoln's day, or will change. So that the blacks, whether inside or outside white society, can become an equal race separately respected.

Our confusion about what the blacks want and what they are likely to get may not be praiseworthy, but it is understandable. Nearly thirty years ago the best available statesmen, historians, soldiers, and politicians sat down in San Francisco to try and gauge the probable future and to direct it. They failed completely to anticipate the two universal movements of our time: the urge of the colored peoples everywhere to be their own rulers; and the urge of country people everywhere to decamp to the cities and the suburbs.

These two coinciding movements have produced a general sense of fear and frustration that once affected—when the American Republic was founded—only a brooding minority of French and English philosophers: the feeling that their own society was overcome by tragic failure, that America was less than the advertised paradise, and that the only pure society existed in some distant island inhabited by noble savages. In the eighteenth century these idealists couldn't sail away there. They could only feed their fantasy on the wishful thinking of explorers. They believed, because they wanted to, in a Brazil where splendid naked women dwelled in perfect amity with men seven feet tall who lived to be one hundred and forty years old. They yearned for "natural religion and natural morality" embodied in creatures innocent of the vices of Christendom; and to their delight, the French explorer Bougainville confirmed the wish with a delirious account of Tahiti. From that moment the idealist trek was on, back to unspoiled nature as the cure for all our woes.

Today we live with more relentless pressures—from crime outside our homes to the specter of the final war. It is no accident, I think, that ours is the great age of tourism, so much so that something less than half the member countries of the United Nations live by it. The promotional come-on is not so fanciful, but just as unreal, as the invitation to Florida held out four hundred years ago by another Frenchman, Jacques Lemoyne, in the first professional painting known to be done in America. The jet plane offers Nirvana and El Dorado in an economy family package. "Getting away from it all," if only for a month, a week, is something all of us can indulge at bargain-basement prices. Computers slot us into available flights. Other computers in travel offices and hotels assign us to a room and private bath on islands we have never seen.

Yet the mirage of the earthly heaven has retreated farther and farther afield. Today, probably for more millions than will ever get there, it is—as it was for the grouchy dreamers of eighteenth-century France—an island in the Pacific. And where more insulated from the madding world than a tiny chain of islands at the exact center of an ocean lapping four continents—Hawaii?

Here, in the winter that George Washington and his ragged army fought to survive at Valley Forge, the first white man stepped ashore and was greeted by the natives as one of their four gods come down to earth. The promise of the tourist literature is that you, too, will feel like Captain Cook. For here are rain forests, and waterfalls, and Bougainville's memento, the bougainvillea; and the dreamy bonus of beautiful, nubile maidens. Such a scene exists on the island of Maui.

But half an hour's flight from Maui is Honolulu, the capital of the fiftieth state. At first glance this city seems a happier and more permanent melting pot than any we have on the mainland. The Polynesians have intermarried freely with most other strains. One notices casually the issue of a Chinese father and an island mother; of a Filipino and a Scot; of a white American father and a Polynesian or Japanese mother. And so far the blacks appear to be more relaxed. Maybe this is the ultimate hope, the next stage in the human family.

But the people of Honolulu are in the same stew as the rest of us. Eighty percent of the islanders have chosen to jam into this city. Planters burn sugar cane for real estate and fill the air with smoke and ash. Surf riders, noticing the signs—"Warning: Polluted Water"—pick out the clean waves. There is choking traffic and urban sprawl and suburban density, and towering skyscrapers, and—"Stop For Guard Check"—the new fear of one's neighbor. Hawaiians had a strong original culture and now preserve a microcosm of it on the east coast of Oahu as a poor Hawaiian's Williamsburg. The more entertaining elements—the music, the flower festivals, the hula, the native drinks—have been diluted and bottled for the tourists who invade the islands in order to feel carefree and safe in the last of the states. Hawaii, far away in the middle of the Pacific, is yet another Western problem. There is no place to hide. And it is time to sum up.

What is fiercely in dispute between the Communist and non-Communist nations today is the quality and staying power of American civilization. Every other country scorns American materialism while striving in every big and little way to match it. Envy obviously has something to do with it, but there is a true basis for this debate, and it is whether America is in its ascendant or its decline.

I myself think I recognize here several of the symptoms that Edward Gibbon maintained were signs of the decline of Rome, and which arose not from external enemies but from inside the country itself. A mounting love of show and luxury. A widening gap between the very rich and the very poor. An obsession with sex. Freakishness in the arts masquerading as originality, and enthusiasm pretending to creativeness. These symptoms are shared by western Europe, though they seem to be milder there only because America has a livelier tradition of self-criticism.

In the past decade America has demonstrated the Roman folly of exercising military might in places remote from the centers of power, and of finding herself so frustrated by the stamina of primitive peoples on their own ground as to fall back on the Roman conclusion that "nothing could reconcile the minds of the barbarians to peace unless they experienced in their own country the calamities of war."

There is, too, the general desire to live off the state, whether it is a junkie on welfare or an airline subsidized by the government: in a word, the notion that Washington—Big Daddy—will provide. And, most disturbing of all, a developing moral numbness to vulgarity, violence, and the assault on the simplest human decencies.

Yet the original institutions of this country still have great vitality: the Republic can be kept, but only if we care to keep it. Much of the social turmoil in America springs from the energy of people who are trying to apply those institutions to forgotten minorities who have awakened after a long sleep.

As for the rage to believe that we have found the secret of liberty in general permissiveness from the cradle on, this seems to me a disastrous sentimentality, which, whatever liberties it sets loose, loosens also the cement that alone can bind any society into a stable compound—a code of obeyed taboos. I can only recall the saying of a wise Frenchman that "liberty is the luxury of self-discipline." Historically those peoples that did not discipline themselves had discipline thrust on them from the outside. That is why the normal cycle in the life and death of great nations has been first a powerful tyranny broken by revolt, the enjoyment of liberty, the abuse of liberty—and back to tyranny again. As I see it, in this country—a land of the most persistent idealism and the blandest cynicism—the race is on between its decadence and its vitality.

There are the woes, which we share with the world, that you can see from your window: overpopulation; the pollution of the atmosphere, the cities, and the rivers; the destruction of nature. I find it impossible to believe that a nation that produced such dogged and ingenious humans as Jefferson and Eli Whitney, John Deere and Ford, Kettering and Oppenheimer and Edison and Franklin, is going to sit back and let the worst happen. There is now a possibility, at least, that nuclear energy can help us to cure incurable diseases, to preserve our food indefinitely, and through breeder reactors, which renew more power in the act of spending it, can actually clean the cities and, let us pray, the oceans. And that would take us over a historical watershed that none of us has ever conceived.

Very often when I was on the road and writing or pondering all this, I found that many old American maxims and idioms, snatches of songs and sententiae floated from the back of my mind into the front of it. When you climb down a rocky cleft in the Great Smokies to a trailblazer's cave or lean into the slamming winds of the prairie, it is not hard to see why "Root, hog, or die" became a warning watchword for several generations. At other times, coming on the records of pioneer husbands who had abandoned their families and joined a railroad gang or headed for the mining country, I found myself spoiled for a choice of their proper epitaph, between "Westward the course of empire," "Pike's peak or bust," or "I love my wife but oh, you kid!" And traveling past the rickety cabins of the black man's back country, and through his scabrous city slums, there often seemed to be only one American theme song: "Sometimes I'm up, Sometimes I'm down, And sometimes I'm almost to the ground."

More often than I care to admit, one of the oldest of American chestnuts seemed newly roasted. It is that line of the Italian immigrant asked to say what forty years of American life had taught him: "There is no free lunch." By now it is a facetious truism, but it is also a profound truth forgotten by the Founding Fathers in the ecstasy of promising everybody life, liberty, and the pursuit of happiness—and it is forgotten again today when committees of Congress imply that transferring $40,000,000 of tax money from the defense budget to revenue sharing will fix everything.

It is a bitterly, and sometimes rousingly, complicated place, this land thrashing over such incessant contradictions as control and permissiveness, the radical young and the conservative middle, the limitlessness of civil rights and the limitations of presidential power. The Swedish sociologist Gunnar Myrdal helped make sense of the constant commotion with his remark to the effect that, while the American tradition is a conservative one, what it has struggled to conserve are often very radical principles indeed.

A still more timely reminder that the government of a free people is meant to be argued about comes from the most famous of American jurists. It gives me, at least, some hope in the outcome of our present conflicts, for it embraces the notion of healthy life as a continuing conflict and strongly suggests that the comfortable impulse to submit and yield to one view of American life or a single instrument of government is an impulse of decay. It is that tremendous line of Justice Oliver Wendell Holmes: "A Constitution is made for people of fundamentally differing views."

Overleaf: *Painted by Jacques Lemoyne, who accompanied a French expedition to Florida in 1564, this bizarre scene purported to show Indians worshipping a column bearing the arms of the King of France. What it really shows is the familiar shape of an old dream—the infinite and readily available abundance of the New World.*

change from a pedant who squealed at a critical adjective about his pet and sent me a fast note saying: "The characterization of Mr. J. will not do." On quite simple matters of fact, both Sir Denis and I nodded from time to time, and I have hastened to correct these errors in the waking hours.

Of all the standard historians, both classical and revisionist, I have been most grateful most often to that venerable Admiral of the Ocean Sea, Samuel Eliot Morison, who threw me a lifeline when I was floundering in whirlpools of competing "facts" and theories. Of later men, Daniel Boorstin whipped up my interest in many vital, though little-noticed, movements. I am specially indebted to him for putting me on to William Ogden, the first mayor of Chicago, and to Frederic Tudor, the first tycoon. And I ought to mention the pleasure and profit I have taken for many years from the works of John Bartlet Brebner, Henry Steele Commager, J. Russell Smith, Mark Sullivan, Frederick Lewis Allen, Gerald Johnson, and J. Frank Dobie, and, more recently, particular volumes by Edmund S. Morgan, James MacGregor Burns, Alvin Josephy, and Merlo J. Pusey. The five volumes of James Truslow Adams' *Dictionary of American History* are a wonderful sheet anchor to have at one's elbow, and both at one's elbow and deep in the hinterland I have learned many things from the incomparable Federal Guides to the States that cannot be found in any other books. I am also grateful to many correspondents between Hawaii and Scotland who questioned or amended or otherwise cleared up statements made in the television series. Among these I am happy to thank Morris Ernst, James Thomas Flexner, J. R. Pole, Audrey Williamson, Peter Farrar, Sheridan A. Logan, John Byrne Cooke, and, especially, Leon J. Salter, an erudite anthropologist who enlightened me (too late, alas, for the film) about "the Bering Strait myth."

None of these worthies is responsible for the errors and frailties that no doubt still burden the text. I must also add the names of several people who are normally excused from a favorable citation, because it is simply supposed to be their daily job to get a television series on the air or a book into the stores. Peter Robeck, of *Time-Life* Films, Inc., was the earliest laborer on the television commodity exchange and finally landed Xerox, the only sponsor I know willing to let a fifty-minute program run fifty minutes without wrenching intervals for the contemplation of the transverse colon or a fluid with the cleaning properties of sulphuric acid. C. Peter McColough, David Curtin, and Robert N. Stahl are to be saluted here.

Once the series was filmed and done with, my next labor was this book, and here there were other people who moved in to match the devotion of the film crews. First among equals is Peter Campbell, who laid out the splendid illustrations of Lord Clark's *Civilisation* and began the same service for me. He was aided at once by Mr. Knopf's indefatigable Anthony Schulte and subsequently by Charles Elliott, Mary Jenkins, and the ever-willing Ann Turner (who should have had enough by the time she had finished directing two of the films). It is not possible to do more than hint here at the encouragement I have taken for a quarter of a century from the friendship and the blunt integrity of the maestro himself, Alfred A. Knopf.

My secretary, Ingrid Luce, bore up with Teutonic phlegm through three years of my unpredictable comings and goings. Finally, it would be churlish to overlook the unsleeping watchfulness over both the film and the book projects of "Justice" Irving Cohen, to whom my debt is payable but insufficient.

No doubt I have omitted, and therefore wounded, some invaluable Mr., Mrs., Miss, or Ms. I claim exemption from a sentence for contempt on the grounds well stated by a learned judge: "Justice is a splendid thing, but you must not expect justice from this life."

The BBC "America" crews:

PRODUCER: Michael Gill.

DIRECTORS: Michael Gill, Ann Turner, Tim Slessor, David Heycock.

CAMERAMEN: Kenneth MacMillan, A. A. Englander, Phil Meheux, John Wyatt.

ASSISTANT CAMERAMEN: Colin Deehan, David Evans, John Walker, Michael Spooner.

SOUND RECORDISTS: Malcolm Webberley, Ron Brown, Colin March, Graham Rodger.

ELECTRICIANS: Stan Palmer, Ken Aylett, David Gorringe, Geoffrey Appleyard, Joe Cooksey, Alan Muhley.

FILM EDITORS: Allan Tyrer, David Thomas, Dan Rae.

ASSISTANT FILM EDITORS: Rosina Pedrick, Derek Towers, Jonathan Crane, Dick Tumbleson, Clive Bell.

DUBBING MIXERS: Alan Dykes, John C. C. Hale.

RESEARCH ASSISTANTS: Joy Curtiss, Sally Evans.

PRODUCERS' ASSISTANTS: Barbara Cannell, Ruth Roberts, Diane Sullivan.

MUSIC ADVISER: Charles Chilton.

MUSIC ARRANGER: Alfred Ralston.

STILLS PHOTOGRAPHER: Roynon Raikes.

ROSTRUM CAMERAMAN: Ivor Richardson.

PICTURE CREDITS

INDEX